Race

to the

Golden Spike

NORTH STAR BOOKS

Race
to the
Golden Spike

PAUL I. WELLMAN

Illustrated by Lorence Bjorklund

HOUGHTON MIFFLIN COMPANY BOSTON
The Riverside Press Cambridge

BOOKS BY PAUL I. WELLMAN

Novels

Broncho Apache
Jubal Troop
Angel With Spurs
The Bowl of Brass
The Walls of Jericho
The Chain
The Iron Mistress
The Comancheros
The Female
Jericho's Daughters
Ride the Red Earth
The Fiery Flower

Histories

Death on the Prairie
Death in the Desert
  (republished together as
  The Indian Wars of the West)
The Trampling Herd
Glory, God and Gold
A Dynasty of Western Outlaws

Reminiscence

Portage Bay

Biography

Stuart Symington

For Younger Readers

Gold in California
Indian Wars and Warriors (East)
Indian Wars and Warriors (West)
Race to the Golden Spike

SOME BOOKS TO READ

THOSE young readers who are interested in the building of the first transcontinental railroad, and in railroading in general, will find numerous books bearing on these subjects in their public or school libraries. Some that the author has found useful are:

Bancroft, Hubert Howe, *History of California.* San Francisco: The History Company, 1888.

Craib, Roderick, *A Picture History of U. S. Transportation.* New York: Simmons-Boardman Books, 1958.

Grinnell, George Bird, *The Fighting Cheyennes.* New York: Charles Scribner's Sons, 1915.

Hornung, Clarence P., *Wheels Across America.* New York: A. S. Barnes & Co., 1959.

Lewis, Oscar, *The Big Four.* New York: Alfred A. Knopf, 1955.

Russell, Charles Edward, *Stories of the Great Railroads.* Chicago: Charles H. Kerr & Co., 1912.

Sabin, Edwin L., *Building the Pacific Railway.* Philadelphia: J. B. Lippincott Co., 1919.

White, Henry Kirke, *History of the Union Pacific Railway.* Chicago: University of Chicago Press, 1895.

CONTENTS

It is unfortunate that many teen-age television fans who devour shoot-'em-up "Westerns" have little if any background in authentic Western history. With very few exceptions the melodramas televised each day grossly exaggerate Western gunplay, gambling, cattle-rustling and other violent aspects of the region.

Violence certainly played its part in our wars against the Indians, our senseless slaughter of the buffalo herds and in the lawless con-duct of some of our western towns. But the creative aspects of Western history, such as the building of the first transcontinental railroad, are largely ignored.

Our West was not built, primarily, by quick-draw "artists." Lewis and Clark, the Mountain Men, the pioneers who opened the Santa Fe and Oregon trails, the settlers who came by covered wagon, and the many decent and quietly brave families who struggled through summers of drought and winters of bitter cold did more for Western history than any gun-man. John Muir, in his fight to save the red-woods and Yosemite, is a greater hero than any western gun fighter, whether outlaw or sheriff.

Paul I. Wellman, who uses authentic and verifiable action in all his exciting books, is also a responsible researcher and historian. His RACE TO THE GOLDEN SPIKE *will hold any reader with its legitimate elements of danger, challenge and courage. But it also furnishes solid, significant and fascinating truth about a labor more impressive than any attempted by Hercules — the incredible construction during the 1860's of a railroad which for the first time tied together two "islands" of American civilization, the East and the West, and which helped to make the United States the unified and dedicated nation which it is today.*

STERLING NORTH
General Editor

TO

MY

WENDY

"If We Live, I've Found the Way"

1

A WARNING CRY: "*Sioux!*"

The general glanced around.

There they were, the deadly Sioux warriors, as though they had sprung from the ground — perhaps a hundred or more wild riders on springy, wiry horses. Their naked legs hung stirrupless, their painted bodies were balanced as if they were parts of the beasts they bestrode. Bow and quiver, lance and rifle were visible, and they were gaudy with paint and fluttering feathers.

Where had those devils come from? No matter, in this country the Sioux were likely to be anywhere.

The general and his escort of a dozen or so mounted men had been scouting along a high ridge of the Black Hills (not those of South Dakota, but a spur of the Rocky Mountains in southeast Wyoming). Cunningly, the hostile Indians had cut them off from the camp of soldiers which was at the foot of these mountains.

The general looked to the right and left. This mountain ridge was wild and precipitous, with cliffs sharp and splintering, their tops bristling with pine and fir trees.

He and his few men would have no chance against those fierce warriors who already had fanned out and begun to ride toward them. How could they escape?

A rifle's keen crack sounded, but the distance was great and the bullet only glanced from a rock and screamed off into space. There was only one thing to do — retreat. Quickly the soldiers turned their horses and rode back along the ridge in the direction from which they had come, looking, looking for some way down to the plains below.

Wild whoops came from behind, as the Indians lashed forward their ponies. Some of the soldiers unslung their carbines and tried a shot or two

to check the hostiles; but everyone knew that escape must be made by racing for life rather than by fighting — if escape was possible at all.

Horses, which had been walking carefully among the trees and boulders, now bounded forward over crevices and fallen tree trunks, making the best speed they could, at the peril of breaking legs or perhaps hurling themselves and their riders over the precipices into the deep, dark gulfs below.

The leader, Major General Grenville M. Dodge, thought only of his responsibility. He must get his men out of the danger into which he had unwittingly led them. He was a keen-eyed man, heavily bearded in the fashion of the time (this was the spring of 1865), so that he looked older than his thirty-four years.

In his career he had seen much service and much danger. Trained as an engineer, he entered the Union army when the Civil War began, distinguished himself for courage and ability to command, won the friendship of General William T. Sherman in the Atlanta campaign, and was made commander of the Department of Missouri.

He was now returning from an expedition trying to pacify the hostile tribes in the Powder River country, and it looked at this moment as though, by misfortune, he had reached the end of his career and perhaps his life.

That morning he had led his command along the foot of these mountains. Though a military officer, he was always an engineer, even on the march with his soldiers, and his eye was ever busy studying the country, with one great dream in his mind — how to find some route by which a railroad could be built across this wilderness.

By instinct and imagination General Dodge was a railroad man, and the mighty plan of a transcontinental railroad was in the air. He knew that one of the greatest obstacles to such a railroad was this very chain of mountains on which he was riding, called the Black Hills because from a distance their forests gave them a black appearance.

He had, therefore, given his troops a rest that morning by the banks of clear-flowing Lodge Pole Creek. With an escort he rode to the top of the ridge, and far along it, wondering if there might not be some way across it for a railroad. Failing to find one, he was returning, when the Sioux appeared, cutting him off from his command.

The Indians were more used to riding in these mountains than the soldiers, and they were gaining in the race. Rifles began to report sharply behind, answered by echoes equally sharp from the opposing cliffs. Bullets whined overhead or struck rocks close at hand. The few shots the fleeing soldiers managed to fire did not take effect, and every man who turned to shoot did so at great risk. A rider in this boulder-strewn and tree-studded route had need to keep his eyes on the way before him.

A mile — two miles — three miles — how much longer could they keep ahead? If any of those bullets from the Indian guns searched out one of the blue-clad horsemen, or even felled his horse, he was lost; and if captured alive, soon dead by torture.

The way suddenly grew steeper. Now the men had to dismount and lead their horses.

Though their progress was slower, they could use their guns to better advantage, and as they reached the top of the ridge, they were still far enough ahead of the Sioux clambering up below so that none of them had yet fallen from a bullet.

Then, all at once, it seemed that the mountain changed slightly in form. Instead of the sheer cliffs, here was a slope. It was rough and broken, choked with trees and rocks, thick bushes, and dead and blasted stumps. Down it ran a stream clogged by beaver dams. Yet it offered the horses footing so that they could be mounted and ridden again.

There was no telling how far this slope went, or whether it might not at any time end in a sheer precipice and leave the men a prey to the Sioux, who were now closing behind them with shrill yells of triumph.

But the eyes of General Dodge suddenly blazed with interest. His practiced gaze had noted the type of rocks and soil, and, above all, dusty game trails of elk and deer. In that moment he almost forgot his peril because of a great hope that sprang up in him — not for life, but for something more important to him than even life itself.

"Boys," he exclaimed, "if we live and save our scalps, I believe I've found the way across the Black Hills!"

His men stared at him in wonder. They did not understand what was in his mind, or his interest in a railroad route. But the slope continued to lead downward, and soon they saw a relief party coming to their aid. Sullenly the Indians fell back toward the upper fastnesses of the mountains, yelling their disappointment at losing their quarry and firing a few last futile shots.

General Dodge and his men were safe.

But before he returned to his main command, he took careful note of a lone pine tree which marked the foot of the grade he had discovered.

Thus, by accident, and owing to what at first seemed the blackest misfortune, the secret of the Black Hills — a way across for the rails — was found, where previously the keenest and most daring minds had failed.

Twelve years earlier, in 1853, when he was only twenty-two years old, Grenville M. Dodge first

had his dream of a railroad across the continent.
In that year he was sent to seek a good point
from which a survey might start at the Missouri
River, and go onward along the Platte Valley —
which was already followed by the famous Overland wagon trail — searching for some route to
reach the golden state of California. He had
never lost that dream.

At Council Bluffs, Iowa, which stands on the
banks of the Missouri, he was visited one day in
1859 by a tall, homely man named Abraham
Lincoln, who was then being talked of as a possible presidential candidate for the new Repub-
lican Party. Lincoln dined with Dodge at the
Pacific Hotel in Council Bluffs. The young engineer, who already had made some important
surveys across the plains, was impressed by the
shrewdness and penetration of the questions asked
by the lawyer from Illinois. That meeting was
to bear fruit.

For decades there had been talk about a railroad across the continent, but at first it was ridi-
culed as impossible. Then came the great gold
strike in California; and what had been thought

impractical began to be discussed soberly. Men put their minds to trying to solve the many problems of finance, labor, and above all, finding the route.

The nation became interested and the government was urged to help build such a railroad. Military exploring expeditions went out trying to find the best way to cross the mountains of the West. In Congress, senators thundered in debate. Several routes were discussed, and each had its backers. Three, however, were most strongly urged.

Senators Sam Houston of Texas and Jefferson Davis of Mississippi — who later became President of the Confederacy — fought for a southern route, by way of El Paso, Texas, and San Diego, California (the route now followed by the Southern Pacific). Senator William H. Seward of New York — later Secretary of State — wanted a northern route, by way of Chicago toward the Columbia River (the route followed now by the Northern Pacific). And Senator Thomas Hart Benton of Missouri favored a central route from St. Louis, through Colorado and on west (the route now followed by the Santa Fe).

All these were good routes, but for years Congress could not agree on which was best. Then Lincoln was elected President in 1860, the great Civil War erupted, and for a time all talk of the railroad was stilled in the rage of that mighty conflict.

But Abraham Lincoln, like George Washington before him, thought constantly of his country, and he believed the best way to unite it and make it strong was through good transportation and communication. Washington worked on a system of canals and turnpikes. But by Lincoln's day railroads had come into being. He took time, from his vast task of conducting the war, to urge a program for building the long-discussed railroad line to the Pacific.

A plan was worked out in Congress whereby the government offered 6400 acres of public lands and a loan of $16,000 to $48,000 — depending on the difficulty of the work — for each mile of completed railroad.

While his armies were reeling before the Confederate forces under General Robert E. Lee, Lincoln signed the act on July 2, 1862.

Then he thought of the young engineer from whom he had obtained so much valuable information at Council Bluffs three years before. Grenville Dodge, the youthful surveyor, was by this time a brigadier general in the Union army. He had been wounded in battle, and had made himself invaluable to the western armies by his skill in building bridges and laying railroad lines. Lincoln summoned General Dodge to Washington.

Once again the two talked long and earnestly. All thought of the southern route, of course, had been dismissed when the Confederate states seceded. The President had the power to fix the point where the new railroad would start, and on the advice of Dodge he chose neither the St. Louis–Colorado route, nor the Chicago–Columbia River route. Instead he selected for the starting place the little hamlet of Omaha, across the Missouri River from Council Bluffs.

Another important matter had to be decided. In 1862 there was great confusion on "gauges"— the distance between the rails on a track. Some railroads had a gauge as wide as 6 feet. Others were as narrow as 3 feet. Because the California railroad builders wanted a 5-foot gauge, Lincoln favored it; but the eastern railroads asked for a gauge of 4 feet 8½ inches. Congress overruled the President, and established that gauge for the transcontinental railroad. It is now the standard gauge not only in this country but in Britain, and allows rolling stock to be shifted from one railroad system to another without difficulty.

With these preliminaries out of the way, offi-

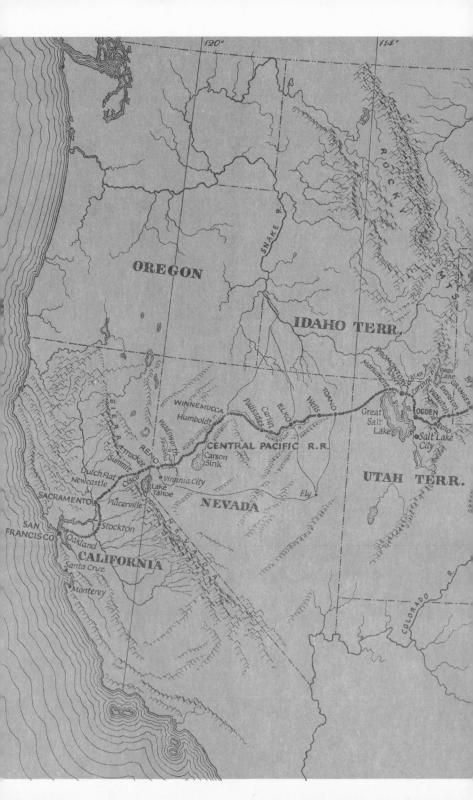

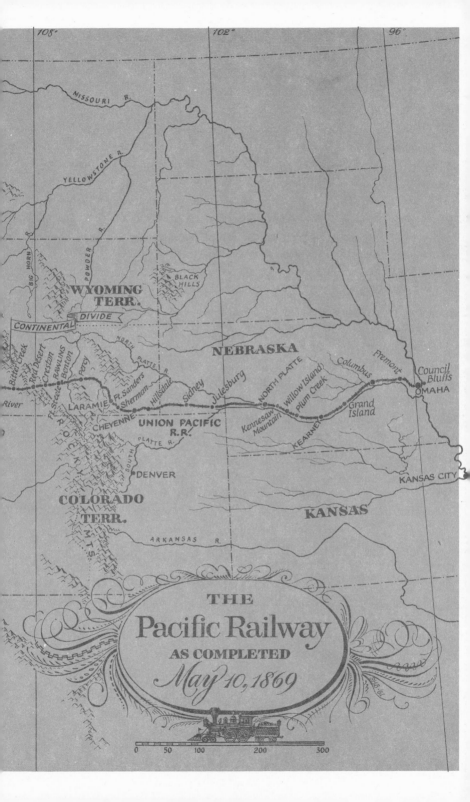

THE
Pacific Railway
AS COMPLETED
May 10, 1869

cials of the newly formed Union Pacific Railroad held a ceremony on the muddy banks of the Missouri at Omaha on December 2, 1863, in which a symbolic spadeful of dirt was turned by Governor Alvin Saunders of the Nebraska Territory, a band played, and speeches were made.

A little more than a month later, January 8, 1864, a similar ceremony took place at Sacramento, in far-off California. This time the earth-breaking spade was wielded by Leland Stanford, who, in addition to being governor of California, was also president of the newly formed Central Pacific Railroad. The speechmaking and band playing, however, were on the same general order as at Omaha.

The two ceremonies marked the beginning of one of the strangest, and most incredible, contests the world ever saw — a race across the continent to build a railroad spanning the empty and un-explored West. Two mighty construction companies would drive, one from the east, the other from the west. Millions on millions of dollars would be expended. Hundreds of men would lose their lives. Tens of thousands would labor in blazing heat or bitter cold. Snows and deserts and warlike Indians would be constant dangers, leading frequently to tragedies.

But somewhere — far out in the wilderness, no man yet knew just where — the two lines would one day meet. And that meeting place would be marked by a last spike of *pure gold.*

The race, however, did not yet begin in earnest, even after earth was broken at Omaha and Sacramento.

There were to be long months of preparation. As yet the railhead of the Union Pacific, building westward from Omaha, had no railroad connection with the East, although a line began slowly creeping from Chicago toward Council Bluffs, just across the Missouri River from Omaha.

In California, the Central Pacific, which was to construct its line eastward from the Pacific Coast, was formed in 1860, when a young engineer named Theodore P. Judah called together a group of Sacramento men. All of them at that time were obscure, though at least four of them would become celebrated. These four, members of Judah's group, were a wholesale grocer named Leland Stanford (later governor of California), a dry-goods dealer named Charles Crocker, and two hardware merchants named Mark Hopkins and Collis P. Huntington.

Judah told them of a survey he had made across the lofty, rugged Sierra Nevada Mountains (usually called the Sierras), east of Sacramento, one of the greatest natural barriers on the continent. To these men, Judah held forth only the thought of gaining control of the traffic from the great new silver mines in Nevada — but he, like Dodge, secretly dreamed of a transcontinental railroad. So the Central Pacific Railroad was organized, and those four storekeepers — Stanford, Crocker, Hopkins, and Huntington — became founders of fortunes so vast that in later years they were known as the "Big Four" of the Pacific Coast.

The Central Pacific in California built a few miles of railroad eastward toward the mountains, but the Union Pacific built not one mile west from Omaha until a second Railroad Act was signed by Lincoln in July, 1864. By that act Congress doubled the land grants and offered its loans on terms so much more attractive that investors began pouring money into the project, and construction began.

At first the Central Pacific was given permission to build only over the Sierras, and an additional 150 miles eastward from those mountains. But in 1866 it was authorized to continue the advance eastward until it met the westward-building Union Pacific.

Each road at once determined to build as many miles across that intervening space as possible. Not only would it be awarded land and government loans for every mile, but each railroad would control the freight and passenger trade over every foot of the lines it owned.

The great battle of titans began in earnest. It was a struggle that kept the attention of the whole world for years, and ended in one of the most dramatic scenes in history.

THE FARSEEING engineer Theodore Judah died in New York, November 2, 1864, from yellow fever contracted while crossing the Isthmus of Panama on a trip east in behalf of the railroad. That was before the work of which he had dreamed was well begun. But he left the job in the hands of four most remarkable men.

Leland Stanford, president of the Central Pacific, was a hearty, forceful personage, who dressed carefully and had a lofty brow and an impressive appearance. He arrived in California in 1852, to aid a brother who started a grocery store in a mining camp. During his life he served for two years as governor of California, was president of the Southern Pacific and Central Pacific railroads, founded a university, and piled up an enormous fortune. To the new railroad he contributed high political and administrative talents.

Collis P. Huntington, vice-president, was a real "Forty-niner," but he devoted only a short time to the muddy pursuit of gold. Instead, he turned his attention to hardware and miners' supplies. Austere, cunning, and determined, he spent most of his time in the East, finding investors to keep construction of the Central Pacific going.

Mark Hopkins, treasurer, was dark, thin, and frail, a shrewd bargainer and manager who was the balance wheel of the organization.

The fourth member of the "Big Four" was Charles Crocker, ·a huge man who normally weighed over 250 pounds and sometimes neared 300. He was boastful and tactless, but he had unlimited courage and tremendous energy which drove other men to great exertions. Born in New York of a poor family, he worked hard from early childhood. But when he was seventeen, his father criticized him by saying he would never be a farmer.

"Do you want me to leave home?" asked the youth.

"Yes, and no," said his father. "Yes, because

you're no use here. No, because I'm afraid you'd
starve to death among strangers."

Crocker left — and he certainly did not starve.
He was the real builder of the Central Pacific Railroad, and became a very rich man like the others
of the "Big Four."

This quartet of men made a powerful combination; and it needed a powerful one to undertake
the task they were launched upon.

A gigantic problem faced the Central Pacific.
Not only did it have to dig and drill its way over
and through extremely lofty and rugged mountains of dense granite rock, almost from the very
start of its construction, but its supplies of iron
and machinery had to be brought by ship from
the eastern states.

Hundreds of thousands of tons of rails and
other hardware, freight cars, passenger cars, and
locomotives were shipped all the way around
Cape Horn, the tip of South America. Voyages
took weeks and even months.

Locomotives of that day were small, weighing
only 20 to 30 tons, compared with later giants

of 200 tons or more. Even so, the freight cost on one shipment of eighteen engines was $84,466.80 — a great sum for that day.

The Central Pacific also had to find men to work on its line. It must be remembered that in those days builders had only the most meager tools with which to work. There were no power shovels, bulldozers, huge earth-movers, mighty cranes, and other great machines that aid road-building now. Everything had to be done by pick and shovel, wheelbarrows, and horse-drawn dump carts.

Dynamite was invented in 1866, but did not come into general use until much later, and for tunneling, the rock either had to be chipped away with chisels and picks, or blasted with inefficient black powder. Literally, the Central Pacific must be built by hand labor.

It took eighteen months to build the first thirty miles from Sacramento to Newcastle, and this was across the coastal level — the easiest part of the route. Now the Sierra Nevada Mountains soared up directly ahead, one of the mightiest ranges on the continent. There must have been grave misgivings in the hearts of the builders when they realized that the really hard part of the task had only just been reached. Better organization was needed. Up to this time several contractors had worked on the road, building short stretches. But at this point, the railroad put the whole great job in the hands of one man — Charles Crocker. Had it not done so, the entire project might have failed, for years at least.

Crocker looked over his task. The route he must follow, surveyed by Judah over the mountains was known as the "Dutch Flat route." It roughly paralleled the old Emigrant Trail by which the Forty-niners came to California. Dutch Flat itself was a mining town, and the surveyed route led through it, up past Donner Lake, where the unfortunate Donner party met its terrible winter fate, and across Donner Pass, to descend by the Truckee River canyon to the plains of Nevada.

The old Emigrant Trail was difficult enough for wagons, or even men mounted on horses. For a railroad it was impossible. Engineers ruled that the maximum grade for standard railroad traffic should not exceed ninety feet to the mile. This meant that a track must seek a way far less steep and crooked than the wagon trail, by means of curves, trestles, tunnels through solid rock, or shelves cut in the faces of towering granite precipices. At times the shelves or ledges were almost as difficult and expensive to make as the tunnels.

For this gigantic task Crocker needed thousands of men — and California labor was very

independent. The gold fields still were produc-
ing precious metal, and in Nevada fabulous riches
were coming from the Comstock Lode and other
silver mines. Often when men took jobs and were
given passes to ride forward to the end of the line
where construction was going on, they merely
got off the work train and walked the short-
ened distance to the silver mines, leaving their
would-be employers furious but helpless.

To add to these difficulties, there was opposition to the building of the railroad across the mountains, some of it bitter, from various sources. San Francisco was jealous of Sacramento and derided the whole project. The Wells Fargo Express Company, the stage lines, including the California, Pioneer, and Overland routes, the Pacific Mail and other steamship companies, small rival railroad promotions, and private toll roads all

fought the Central Pacific, because they thought they would lose business if it ever was completed. There even was an ice concern — the Sitka Ice Company, which brought ice by ship from Alaska at five cents a pound — that feared ice would be brought from the snowy and icy summits of the Sierras if the railroad ever reached them. All these threw themselves into the fight against the Central Pacific, making it difficult at times to get the capital needed for the work.

Yet in spite of all these discouragements, the Central Pacific continued to build. Crocker's job was backbreaking. The reason it took eighteen months to build from Sacramento to Newcastle was principally because he could not get or keep men. Sacramento, Stockton, and San Francisco were combed for laborers.

Grappling with the problem, President Stanford in 1864 petitioned the War Department to send out 5000 Confederate prisoners of war, to be put to work under a guard of Union soldiers. But this proposal for what amounted to "slave labor" was not viewed with favor by Lincoln or the War Department.

Somehow Crocker found crews. Nobody who applied for a job was turned down, but all too few applied, and those who did were of such poor quality that they only added to the profane language of the bosses up front. Even old men and boys were hired. Men who went to work often left within a few days or weeks for the beckoning silver mines.

Yet Crocker's tremendous energy somehow kept the work going and by March, 1865, the axes of men clearing trees, shouts of teamsters driving dump carts, and the roar of black-powder blasts, were heard as far as Illinoistown, and the Central Pacific, pushing ever eastward, was operating fifty-six miles of railroad.

But the big job was still ahead, and Crocker racked his brain for some way to solve it. He had a personal servant, a Chinaman named Ah Ling, who for years had proved faithful, capable, and industrious. Ah Ling's abilities started Crocker thinking in a new direction.

The gold strikes had brought tens of thousands of Chinese to California. Though the white miners refused to let them mine the regular fields, they patiently washed gravels that already had been worked over in abandoned placers, for the pitifully small amount of gold remaining. Because they ate simply and cheaply, they could live and labor where white men would have starved.

Crocker began to observe these people. He noticed that the Chinese were in their gravel pits long before white men rolled out of bed. They worked until it was too dark to see, long after white men had quit for the day. The combination of Ah Ling and the Chinese coolies gave Crocker an idea. What about using Chinese to build the railroad?

When he made the suggestion he found strong opposition. His construction superintendent, J. H. Strobridge, would have nothing to do with the idea at first. He pointed out that average Chinese men weighed probably no more than 110 pounds. They ate rice, which, he said, could not be strengthening. The very idea of putting these underweight weaklings to work building a railroad over the Sierras was, to him, preposterous.

But Crocker insisted, and at last Strobridge reluctantly agreed to try a crew of fifty Chinese.

The gang of coolies was gathered, placed in freight cars, and hauled to the end of the line. There they got off, quietly made camp, cooked a meal of dried cuttlefish and rice, and went to sleep on the ground.

At the first light of dawn they were up, picks, shovels, and wheelbarrows busy. All day they labored with hardly a rest, and Strobridge, who expected them to collapse under such toil, revised his opinions. When night came and he surveyed the work they had done, he was both astonished and delighted.

More Chinese were sent for at once. Within six months, 2000 of them, clad in the blue cotton denim of the Orient and wearing huge basket hats that looked almost like umbrellas, were swarming like ants along the railroad, making cuts and filling grades at a rate beyond the hopes of anyone. Eventually at least 10,000 coolies were employed on the work of construction and maintenance of the railroad.

Some white men resented the coming of the Chinese. But they soon saw that the coolies lived in their own camps, cooked their own food, and were polite and docile. Their advent, further-more, meant promotion for most of the white workers, who were relieved of pick-and-shovel work, and became teamsters, powder men, stone-masons, and gang foremen. The Chinese had won a real place for themselves.

Crocker now redoubled his exertions. Up and down the line he stormed, bellowing, driving his men to greater efforts. The Chinese half worshiped, half feared him. He was "Cholly Clocky" to them — their pronunciation of Char-ley Crocker. When he roared, they jumped; and he roared often, so they worked, if possible, even faster.

"I used to go up and down that road in my car like a mad bull," he later told George Ban-croft, the historian, "stopping along the way wherever there was anything amiss, and raising old Nick with the boys." Another time, he re-lated with pride, "Everyone was afraid of me. I was just looking around for someone to find fault with all the time."

But he had his kindly side too. He insisted on paying his workers himself, because payday gave them such pleasure. With two leather bags heavy with coin, he would ride his big sorrel mare into the midst of a gang, take out a paper, call off the names of the men, and as each stepped forward he would take coins from the bags — gold on one side, silver on the other — and drop the pay into the outstretched hand of the grinning coolie. This happened once a month, and he sometimes carried 150 pounds of gold and silver to a given camp.

By the start of 1866 there were 6000 of the Chinese at work, and they were beginning to be called "Crocker's Pets," a name which clung to them as long as the construction lasted.

By this time they had reached the place where the really tough construction began. The basket-hatted and denim-clad figures attacked the work with their usual swarming industry. With picks and shovels they pecked at the granite rock, their faces expressionless, their toil never ceasing.

At many places the picks could not penetrate because the granite was too hard. The Chinese carried blasting powder — a seventy-pound keg on each end of a bamboo pole balanced across the shoulders — up dangerously high and narrow paths along the cliff sides.

Other Chinese were busy with hammer and drill, for Crocker found them adept at this back-breaking labor. When the holes were drilled, the powder was poured in and sealed, the fuses lit, and the crews fell back until the shattering boom of the blast echoed in the canyon. Then, in long

lines, the coolies with their wheelbarrows carried broken rock and gravel and dumped it down the side of the gorge.

Crocker used as many as 500 kegs of powder a day, and still he called for more.

The Chinese refreshed themselves with sips of tea. They ate rice and dried fish, and slept on the ground. They received a wage of two dollars a day and they were always on the job. Crocker was happy with them.

Behind the graders came the track-layers. These usually were white men and some of them were very skillful. Following the track-layers came Crocker's construction trains — flatcars, pushed by locomotives, carrying ties, rails, spikes, construction iron, lumber, powder, food, drink, and more men. The supply of ties was no problem for the Central Pacific, as it was to be for the Union Pacific. The roadway was through huge forests and axmen kept the track-layers well supplied. But there was no time to season these ties. Many of them were laid not only green, but with the bark still on.

The first really appalling obstacle encountered

was when the right-of-way came flush against a mountain of pure granite, with a sheer beetling cliff which dropped straight down for a thousand feet with not a sign of a foothold. The only way to get around it was literally to cut a roadbed into the face of that great cliff.

The Chinese were not daunted. They examined the cliff — which was dubbed "Cape Horn" by white workers — and then set about weaving baskets of thin strips of wood. The baskets were strong enough to hold a man — at least a small Chinaman. But when lowered over the cliff by ropes, with men in them, they spun around dizzily, or tipped when an edge happened to catch on a rough place on the granite face, and the passenger had to cling to the ropes to keep from being hurled to his death in the awful depths below.

Nevertheless the Chinese accepted the danger. Hanging between the skies and the splintered rock of the bottom of the gorge hundreds of feet straight down under them, they chipped with hammers and stonecutter's chisels to form a ledge. Some of them died when their ropes slipped or became unfastened, letting shrieking wretches plunge downward to be dashed to pieces at the foot of the cliff. But the others did not quit. They merely took care that their moorings were stronger, and continued to cut at the stubborn granite.

At last by sheer patience and at never-ending risk, they succeeded in chiseling out a very narrow and dangerous ledge — a mere foothold on which men could balance themselves. But the foothold, small and perilous as it was, gave them better purchase for their work than the swinging baskets. All day the clink of hammers and chisels sounded, with now and then the rattle of stone chips falling down over the cliff. At length the Chinese deepened their ledge to a shelf wide enough to permit the laying of track and the passage of cars, a roadbed literally cut by hand through some of the hardest granite in the world.

In later years when trains crept cautiously along this shelf, around the curve of the cliff, passengers, although safe in their seats, gazed down with horror from their car windows into the abyss, hardly thinking of the brave men who

cut the way with infinite labor, and sometimes at the cost of their lives.

By May the track-layers were working on the shelf chiseled out by the Chinese. The town of Dutch Flat was reached in July, 1866.

Dutch Flat, a mining town, was of strategic importance. From it the Central Pacific opened a wagon trail which connected with the stage and freighting road between Placerville and Virginia City, and thus brought much traffic to the new railhead.

That wagon route brought a storm of criticism. Enemies of the company screamed that the Central Pacific never intended to go any farther; that it would rest with its terminus at Dutch Flat to drain business from the Nevada silver country. Newspapers began to refer to the "Dutch Flat swindle," referring to the stock sold by the railroad in order to build to that point.

Other critics said it was obvious that the railroad could make no further progress, even if it tried. This was based on the fact that the lofty and snowy caps of the Sierras almost overhung the mining town and it appeared impossible to surmount them.

But these people did not reckon on the courage and skill of the officers of the Central Pacific, or its men, above all "Crocker's Pets."

Hardly pausing for breath at Dutch Flat, the grading crews pressed on, Crocker roaring up and down the line. Slowly the iron rails thrust onward and upward, past historic mining camps with strange names: Gold Run, Red Dog, You Bet, Little York.

Now difficulties that would have disheartened most men faced Crocker. The plan of the route called for tunnel after tunnel — most of them 1000 feet or longer. Deep cuts also had to be made. And all this, in the upper ridges of the Sierras, must be carved through solid stone of a hardness nobody had expected when the work began.

Picks and chisels flattened their points against the granite. When, after backbreaking toil, holes were drilled into it and powder placed in the holes to blast the rock, the explosive when ignited spurted back through the drill holes, leaving the stone unbroken.

In despair Crocker turned to a compound of which he had heard but had never seen — nitroglycerin. The explosive had been widely heralded as extremely powerful. Crocker imported a chemist, named Swansen, from the Nobel laboratories in Sweden — where Alfred Nobel in that year, 1866, would invent dynamite by combining certain materials with nitroglycerin. Swansen said he could, given the right elements, manufacture the tricky substance on the spot.

Little was known about nitroglycerin. Not even the chemist could speak with authority on its behavior. Sometimes there were premature explosions, for the substance blew up violently at the slightest jar. When such an explosion occurred there was nothing left of either the evidence or the witnesses. The final climax came when Strobridge, the construction superintendent, lost an eye in an unexpected blast, although he was at a distance from it. After that no more nitroglycerin was used.

The experiment seemed to sour Crocker, for later when an inventor appeared with a steam rock-drill, although he was eagerly welcomed by Stanford and others, Crocker and Strobridge would have nothing to do with him or his device. They wanted no more newfangled gadgets. The tunnels — and there were fifteen of them all told — continued to be chipped out by hand, with the help of black powder when it could be used.

Had they tried the steam drill, they would have found it very practical, for in a couple of years it was in general use all over the world. Crocker's refusal to try the device cost his company a needless $2,000,000, and lost months of valuable time which enabled the rival Union Pacific, coming west from Omaha, to build hundreds of miles of railroad which otherwise they would not have had time to build.

When the Central Pacific reached Cisco, California, on November 23, 1866, ninety-two miles of railroad had been constructed from Sacramento, much of it hewn from solid rock and pronounced the most difficult work of its kind in the history of the world. It might have been considered a good place to stop, for winter was coming on, and winters in the high Sierras are fierce. But just at this time news came of the great strides of the Union Pacific coming across the plains from far to the east. Crocker decided to plunge on, winter or no winter.

Bought With Blood and Sweat

WE MUST NOW, for a time, leave the Central Pacific hacking its way with desperate strokes through the granite buttresses of the Sierras, and look far to the east to see how the rival Union Pacific was progressing. It was not until July 10, 1865, that the first rail of the Union Pacific was laid at the starting point, Omaha. And real progress did not begin until General Dodge was released from his military duties in 1866, to become chief engineer of the railroad.

The men who were to build the Union Pacific westward were as varied in personality and character as those who constructed the Central Pacific eastward from California. Behind the scenes, grappling with the problems of financing, were shrewd men like Oakes Ames, a daring speculator; Dr. Thomas C. Durant, a dreamer and promoter;

and Sidney Dillon, a wily man of money.

But the actual construction was in the hands of General Grenville Dodge, bearded, strenuous, an engineer who understood the problems of both building and military discipline. Under him, as construction superintendent, was a driving fury, General Jack Casement, short, lean, and hard. General Casement's brother Dan was at the rear of construction, spurring the forwarding of supplies and men; General Jack was at the front as the line progressed, fighting for every mile of rails laid; and General Dodge was up and down the route tirelessly, encouraging, scolding, solving problems, inspiring.

When the Union Pacific's difficulties are considered, they almost seem greater than those of the Central Pacific. True, a large part of its mileage would be laid across flat plains country, far easier to build in than mountain country. But the Union Pacific must encounter mountains at the end of its stretch, instead of at the beginning.

Meantime it faced transportation problems almost as serious as its rival's. All of its materials — iron rails, hardware, locomotives, cars, supplies, even wooden ties at first — had to be brought by water, using steamboats on the Mississippi-Missouri river system.

One of the great needs of the Union Pacific which did not face the Central Pacific in the same measure, was for timber for ties and trestles. Over the entire proposed route from Omaha to the Black Hills there were hardly any large trees, except cottonwoods, which would rot in two or three years. Timber grew in abundance in the

Black Hills; but first the Black Hills must be reached, and they were hundreds of miles away.

The Union Pacific contracted for more than six million ties — some coming from as far east as Pennsylvania and New York — as well as transporting more than 300,000 tons of rails, together with locomotives, cars, and other equipment, brought by river and assembled in Omaha.

The muddy and treacherous Missouri River could be navigated for only about three months

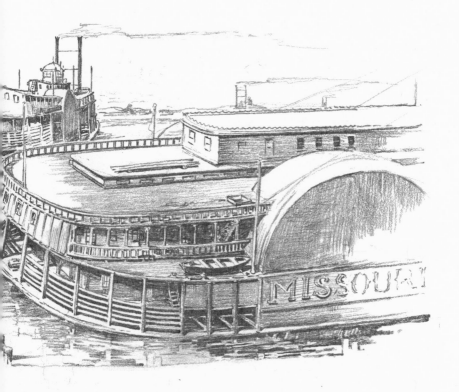

a year, when the river was in freshet, so that steamboats would have enough water under their keels to progress, which further complicated the problem.

Later, in 1867, the Chicago & Northwestern Railroad did reach Council Bluffs from Chicago. But even then there was no bridge over the river, and materials had to be conveyed across to Omaha by ferry in warm weather, and over the ice in winter.

As Edwin L. Sabin wrote: "The Union Pacific was like a cantilever bridge, begun in midstream and teetering out through vacancy for the farther bank. It commenced nowhere; it reached forward without visible support, and where it would end was uncertain."

A problem in some ways as serious as transportation, was the hostility of the Indians on the plains. Very early this danger was felt when advance parties were attacked.

Nevertheless, whatever the obstacles, the Union Pacific, under Dodge, threw its full strength into the giant building contest, and the historic race was on.

First, surveys must be made, the route decided.

Gold had been struck in the Rocky Mountains of Colorado, and the Union Pacific wished if possible to tap that rich area, just as the Central Pacific wanted to reach the Nevada silver fields. Yet, from the first, General Dodge knew his line could not go through Denver.

The practicable route could not even follow the old Overland Trail, except here and there. One of the most strategic passes over the mountains, for a railroad line, had been discovered by Dodge himself in that old Indian encounter of 1865.

Almost his first act as chief engineer was to send James A. Evans, with a surveying party, to verify his estimate of what he called "Lone Tree Pass." Evans, with his transits and chains, proved that the pass was all that Dodge hoped for, and it was named "Evans Pass." But later the name was changed again to "Sherman Pass," in honor of General Sherman, Dodge's old commander and great friend.

Though Evans and his party made their survey and returned in safety, they were almost the last to be so fortunate. The Union Pacific, moving

westward across the plains, had to face the enmity
of the warlike tribes of Indians whose territories
the rails must cross — Sioux, Cheyennes, Arap-
ahoes, and others.

The Central Pacific, in the far West, headed off
Indian interference by making treaties and giving
gifts to the Paiutes and Shoshones with whom it
came into contact. But these were desert tribes,
living in want, and they were never a serious
danger.

Far different were the proud horsemen of the plains, who were murderous and brave, looked upon war as the most honorable occupation for any man, and saw very early that the coming of the railroad meant an end to their way of life.

Even before Dodge took charge, the Indians made known their resentment of the white man. During the year 1865, while Dodge was still in the army, Cheyennes destroyed Julesburg, one of the way points planned for the railroad, burned several stage stations and ranches, and ambushed a military force at Platte Bridge, in Wyoming Territory. In these raids and fights they killed thirty-five soldiers and twenty-two civilians, besides carrying off two women and a child into captivity.

Knowing this, it took brave men to go out on surveying parties in 1866 and 1867. Yet they went.

Far ahead of construction, out in the Indian country, their daily lives were perilous. Surveying could only be done by stringing the crews out, and this made them particularly easy to attack. Before long it became apparent that they must have military escorts. Yet, even with soldiers to guard them, every foot they traveled was dangerous.

A few examples will show what happened.

In May, 1867, a surveying party was working six miles east of the present city of Cheyenne, Wyoming, headed by L. L. Hills, who had assisted Evans in his survey of the Lone Tree Pass.

Suddenly the wild yells of a Sioux war party were heard. The painted skulkers had been stalking the surveyors, and now they burst into view. Hills fell dead at the first fire, and for a while it looked as if the whole party would be ridden down and killed.

But a youth named J. M. Eddy, not yet twenty-one years old, seized a rifle and shot at the oncoming warriors, bringing one to the ground. This caused the Sioux to pause, and in those moments of hesitation young Eddy took cool command of the other men, all of whom were older and presumably more experienced than he. Arranging them in a skirmish line, each with a rifle, he began a cautious retreat toward the camp, six miles away.

Now the Sioux again charged forward and swirled about the little group. But Eddy saw to it that while some of his men fired, others kept their shots in reserve.

The Indians had hoped for a surprise and panic, and the easy taking of scalps. The quick thinking of the boy in the crew prevented that.

The Sioux could fight bravely when they thought it worth while, but now they knew they could not hope to wipe out the surveyors without suffering losses themselves. To have good braves killed for the sake of a few scalps did not appeal to them.

So they contented themselves with skirmishing at rather long range, until the firing was heard at the camp and reinforcements came to help the retreating surveyors. Then the Indians rode off. They had one scalp (Hills's), and they bore away one wounded warrior. Eddy had saved the rest of the surveying party.

A report of this was made to General Dodge, naming a certain J. M. Eddy as the hero of the episode. Dodge, of course, knew nothing about Eddy, but he asked headquarters at Omaha to

give him the young man's status. Shortly he learned that Eddy was an axman — one of the most subordinate jobs on a surveying crew — and also that he had fought in the Sixteenth Army Corps of the Union army during the Civil War.

Here was something of interest — General Dodge had commanded the Sixteenth Corps himself!

He was about to start west on an inspection

trip, and he wired Eddy to meet him at Lodge Pole Creek, near the scene of his brave deed. When the young man presented himself, the general questioned him and found that he had enlisted in an Illinois regiment when he was sixteen and had fought under Dodge in several campaigns.

Much pleased, the general at once promoted him in the surveying service, and thereafter kept

track of him. Before he was through with railroading, J. M. Eddy was widely known as the
general manager of the Texas & Pacific Railroad.

General Dodge had much bad news that trip.
To the west another surveying party had been
struck by the Sioux.

The leader was Percy T. Browne, another of
Evans's assistants. He had been sent to "develop
the country from Fort Sanders [near present-day
Laramie] to the Green River."

Browne knew it was a highly dangerous mis-
sion, but he started out, with a squad of soldiers
as escort. Fifty-five miles from Fort Sanders,
on the evening of May 12, his camp was suddenly rushed by the Sioux.

A small party, out gathering wood, led by
Stephen Clark, a mere youth, was cut off and
slaughtered. Sergeant Clair, of the escort, was
also killed, and several men wounded. But the
survivors took shelter and beat off the Sioux in an
all-night fight.

Browne took the bodies of the slain back to

Fort Sanders, and secured men to replace them. Though he was fully aware now of the deadly hate of the Sioux, he had orders. So, with a strong military escort this time, he pushed across the Continental Divide to what was called the Red Desert, in southwest Wyoming Territory.

There he found his maps untrustworthy. With eight troopers he rode on ahead of the main party, to try to discover landmarks on which he could rely.

The buttes and the soil were red, with little vegetation save sagebrush; and water, when it was found, was bitter with alkali. Occasionally a gaunt antelope was seen, or a wandering coyote. Of birds there were almost none, except for a black buzzard now and then wheeling far above in the cloudless sky.

Yet in this stark and apparently vacant desert, Indians lurked, watching the little troop of riders, from hiding places in the buttes.

At noon on July 23, whooping like fiends, 300 Sioux swirled out in a cloud of red dust from a defile between two ruddy buttes.

Browne and his troopers managed to reach a small hillock. There they dismounted and sought to defend themselves. They were nine against 300, but as if at ease on some target range, the soldiers drew beads on the careering savages, and opened fire.

Some feathered warriors spun out of their saddles into the red dust.

With losses, the Sioux drew back. But then they surrounded the hillock and kept up a long-range fire.

At dusk Browne was struck in the stomach by a leaden slug. He knew his wound was mortal.

Meantime the Sioux, after stampeding all the horses of the party, began to draw away as night fell. If ever, this was the time for the white men to escape. Browne called his companions to him and told them to leave him and make for the stage line on foot.

The men refused. Making a litter from their guns and a blanket, they lifted him into it, and headed off in the darkness, taking turns carrying the wounded man. Though they knew the general direction to take, they did not know at what moment they might stumble into an Indian ambush or encampment.

Luck was with them. Without seeing a foe, they arrived next morning at a stage station called LaClede. Their leader died there.

Other parties were attacked and men lost. And there were perils aside from the Indians.

Near present-day Creston, Wyoming, a company of soldiers saw at a distance some figures crawling on hands and knees. At first they thought they were Indians attempting to steal up on them, but soon they made out that the creeping people were white men.

It was the surveying party of Thomas H. Bates. The men had run out of water in the desert, and a poison lake, from which their horses drank, killed the animals and almost killed some of the surveyors. Using a compass, Bates struck a line due east, hoping to find help. But for three days he and his men had not tasted water. Their faces were twisted in the agony of thirst, their tongues were swollen and black; they were dragging themselves forward on hands and knees by sheer will power.

The rescuers reached them, gave them water in judicious amounts and at judicious intervals so as not to kill them, and brought them safely to the railhead.

Still another group was trapped for two weeks in the mountains by heavy snows, and almost starved to death before they could make their way out. In those days it took real men to run the survey lines for the Union Pacific.

Yet, in spite of all difficulties and dangers, the surveyors laid out the route: west from Omaha, following the Platte River, to the Black Hills in southwest Wyoming; over the former Lone Tree (now Sherman) Pass, down to the Laramie plains; still west across the Red Desert, over the Green River and through the Wasatch Mountains by Weber Pass; on around the northern end of Great Salt Lake, and beyond.

That was the way the grading crews went, followed by the track-layers, with the stakes set before them by the heroic surveying parties. This route left Denver and Salt Lake City off to one side, and created disappointment and anger in those places. But it was the one practicable route to follow if the railroad was to span the continent in a line as direct as was necessary.

Across the Indian Country

IN SPITE OF the troubles of the surveyors, General Sherman, who was then in command of the army, did not think the actual building of the railroad would be perilous. To his brother, a congressman, he wrote: "No particular danger need be apprehended from the Indians . . . So large a number of workmen distributed along the line will introduce enough whiskey to kill off all the Indians within 300 miles of the road."

He soon found out he was in error, as appeals for help came to the War Department. Not only were the Indians still threatening, but the whiskey killed off about as many workers as it did Indians.

The difficulty of the enterprise was expressed by Oakes Ames, one of the financial backers of the Union Pacific, who wrote:

To undertake the construction of a railroad, at any price . . . in a desert and
unexplored country, its line crossing three
mountain ranges at the highest elevations
yet attempted on this continent, extending
through a country swarming with hostile
Indians, by whom locating engineers and
conductors of construction trains were repeatedly killed and scalped at their work;
upon a route destitute of water, except as
supplied by water trains, hauled from 100
to 150 miles to thousands of men and animals engaged in construction; the immense
mass of material, iron, ties, lumber, provi-
sions and supplies necessary to be trans-
ported from 500 to 1500 miles — I admit
might well, in the light of subsequent history, be regarded as the freak of a madman,
if it did not challenge the recognition of a
higher motive.

In the years following the Civil War, many
veterans were out of work. From these the Union
Pacific recruited most of its labor. As a matter

of fact most of the men were Irish immigrants, who had gone into uniform and fought well during the war. They were uneducated but knew how to work hard. There were others also, including not a few Confederate veterans, who were nicknamed "Galvanized Yankees."

It was well that these men knew army life and were accustomed to danger and the smell of gunpowder, because the farther the railhead traveled from the base of supplies, the greater and more constant was the danger of Indian raiders.

General Dodge wrote later, of the years while the track was being laid:

> Every mile had to be run within range of the musket. In making the surveys numbers of our men, some of them the ablest and most promising, were killed; and during the construction our stock was run off by the hundred, I might say by the thousand; and our cars and stations and ranches burned. Graders and track-layers, tie-men and station-builders, had to sleep under guard, and have gone to work with their picks and shovels and other mechan-

ical tools in one hand and the rifle in the
other, and often had to drop one to use
the other.

From the start the whole system of work was
organized along military lines. Officials of the
company were, by actual army rank, generals,
colonels, and majors. In the surveying crews were
captains, lieutenants, and former enlisted men.
Work squads usually were under an ex-sergeant
as foreman. Army shirts and trousers worn by the
veterans gave a military appearance to things.
Sometimes platoons of laborers would shoulder
their shovels and picks in the morning and march
off to the job in formation, their sergeant-foremen
crying, "Left, right, left, right, hep, hep, hep — "
as they had called to keep their men in step
during the campaigns of the late war.

Once, when a report came to General Dodge
that Indians were attacking a freight train a few
miles down the track, he rallied the men who
were available, and discovered that they all
obeyed the order, "Fall in." Deploying them as
skirmishers, he recaptured the train, or what was

left of it, driving the Indians off. Of these men he said: "They went forward as steadily and in as good order as we had seen the old soldiers climb the face of Kenesaw [Mountain] under fire."

Following the stakes set by the surveyors and with everything going by orders in the good old army way, the grading crews led the construction. With picks and shovels and horse-scoops, they made cuts and fills, keeping the grade at the

exact level the transits decreed. Across streams and rivers they built wooden bridges, sometimes lofty trestles made of timbers brought from hundreds of miles away.

Every bit of this was under conditions of war. As they pushed the grade farther and farther into the Indian country, the men built what they called "prairie monitors"— after the flat-decked little warships with rotating turrets that had become popular during the recent conflict. These

were simply dugouts, sometimes roofed over with
sheet iron. Each sheltered four or six men, if
Indians attacked. The ex-soldiers knew well how
to make such shelters in quickest time: they had
made them in the battles before Vicksburg, and
in the Wilderness campaign, and at the siege of
Petersburg.

Behind the grading crews — which were sometimes as much as a hundred miles ahead of construction — came the tie-men, placing the ties,
followed by the rail-layers.

The scene at the railhead was one of never-
ending excitement and drama. Up would puff
a construction train, halt with a noisy clatter of
brakes, and with a sound of thunder dump its
load of ties or rails.

Along the new-laid track from up ahead would
come horse-drawn rail trucks, the animals galloping with the empty trucks, which rolled on the
rails. Into a truck would be loaded forty rails,
and away they would go — the horses now
hitched to the other end of the trucks — pulling
toward the grade ahead. Empty trucks on the

track would be tipped over on one side to let the loaded trucks pass. Then they would be replaced on the tracks and their drivers would whoop the horses to speed as they hurried for a new load.

Waiting for the loaded trucks would be two rail-laying squads — five men to a squad — one group on the right, the other on the left. Two rails at once would be plucked free by iron pincers in the hands of these men, and carried forward to where the ties had already been laid.

Poised there for a moment, the order "Down!" would come from the rail bosses. At the word, each rail was lowered, and its end forced into the "chair"— an iron block forming a socket or clutch to hold the rail end-to-end with the preceding rail, on the tie.

Up ahead the two new rails would be set their exact width apart by gaugers, who saw to it that the 4 feet 8½ inches, "measured at right angles at a point ⅝ of an inch below the top of the rail," was rigidly maintained.

"Ready!" would call the gauger. The chief spikers swung their sledges, the spikes bit into the wood, and another pair of rails was laid.

So rapid and expert did this process become, that the work was reckoned as follows: thirty seconds to each pair of rails; two rail lengths to the minute; three blows to each spike; ten spikes to the rail; 400 rails, 4000 spikes, and 12,000 sledge-hammer blows to each mile.

Sometimes, for added speed, only every other tie was laid when the rails came down. As the rail trucks pushed forward, crews followed them, inserting extra ties and spiking them home.

Spikers never seemed to miss a blow, tie-handlers and rail-layers never seemed to make a false motion. Supply trains unfailingly brought up new loads of rails, spikes, chairs, bolts, and ties.

It was a titanic task. The magnitude and precision of the work inspired awe in all who saw it. Later, Robert Louis Stevenson, the great poet and novelist, wrote: "It seems to me, I own, as if this railway were the one typical achievement of the age in which we live."

When on December 11, 1866, construction was halted by winter, the astounding total of 260

miles of track had been laid in eight months —
an average of more than a mile a working day.
The 100th meridian (which, at 247 miles from
Omaha, was marked by a wooden arch) was
passed. The railhead was at North Platte, Nebraska, 293 miles from Omaha, and the end of
track was twelve miles farther on.

That winter of 1866–67, while the track crews
inhabited it, North Platte roared "wide open" day
and night, with its tent saloons and gambling
dens, its frequent knifings and shootings, its growing graveyards and its lynchings. The town had
not even existed on November 1, 1866, but by
November 22, the same month, it had mush-
roomed to a population of 1000 persons.

Wrote one observer, of North Platte in that
winter:

> Everything and everybody bound west-
> ward stopped here en route; Mormon emi-
> grants, Idaho settlers, Montana gold-seek-
> ers, Overland travelers waiting for a seat
> on the stage for Denver and Salt Lake;
> plains and mountain freighting outfits by
> the dozen, their hundreds of unshaven bull-

whackers ruffling through the streets; gamblers of the North, South, and East, reveling in "flush times" come again; soldiers, remittance men, second sons; down-at-heels lawyers, doctors, clergymen, in the guise of jacks-of-all-trades; and tenderfeet plunged into the glamor cast by swagger of body and display of holstered belt. Every building seemed to house a saloon, and every saloon was a den.

And always the Indians were a threat and a menace.

Early in 1866, Red Cloud, a great Sioux Chief, sent a warning that the railroad must not be built, in these words:

"We do not want you here. You are scaring away the buffalo."

Yet at first the Indians seemed more curious than destructive. They rode up on their ponies to watch with astonishment the labor of the tracklayers. Then, as it gradually came over them that their very existence was threatened by this new wonder of the white man, they became dangerous.

They began with petty thefts, increasing to larger ones. Then they started stampeding horse and mule herds and attacked construction crews and trains. Only the simplicity of the savages and their lack of organization kept the losses from being far heavier than they were. Those losses were heavy enough, in lives and property, as it was.

Fire and Gun and Lance

5

THE YEAR 1867 dawned bloodily as the Union Pacific resumed building westward toward the mountains.

This was the year when the plains Indians made a supreme effort to stop the march of civilization. All along the Smoky Hill Emigrant Route through Kansas and Colorado, and all along the Overland Trail through Nebraska, "stage hands fought from sod walls and galloping coaches for their lives." South of the Union Pacific, a different line, the Kansas Pacific, which only sought to build from Kansas City to Denver, found its progress entirely blunted, impossible to maintain against the Indian menace.

Soldiers campaigned against the warlike tribes — Hancock, Custer, and others, with their hard-riding troopers, including Major Frank North and his Pawnee scouts, friendly Indians who fiercely fought their hereditary enemies, the Sioux and Cheyennes.

And yet the hostile warriors continued to swoop down on construction camps, run off horses and mules by herds, and kill men when they could. The Union Pacific did its best to meet the danger.

Work trains that year were made into "forts on wheels," with living quarters double-walled and sand-packed for protection against bullets and arrows, and loopholes to fire through. Every work or passenger car was equipped with rifles and ammunition. Freight train cabooses likewise were strengthened. Engineers and firemen had guns within quick reach in every cab, and brakemen all wore revolvers at their belts. Rifles were standard equipment for graders, station keepers, and track laborers.

Yet, with all these precautions, trouble grew and lives were lost.

Sometimes the Indians, who knew nothing of the power of trains, tried laughable — though often tragic — tricks. One warrior, hoping to throw a speeding engine off the track, lassoed the smokestack, the other end of the rope being tied about his waist. Said a newspaper account of the episode, "He succeeded in roping the smokestack, but the Indian is dead."

Even more disastrous was another experiment. Some Indians tried to stop the "Iron Horse" by stretching across the track a rawhide rope, fastened to the ponies on which they were mounted. The engine, of course, rushed on, overthrowing and killing the ponies and their riders.

Thereafter the Indians grew more cautious. Sometimes they would race a speeding train, peppering the engine and cars with their rifles.

Then, one day, an old squaw hit upon a better idea. She studied the Iron Horse, and saw that it traveled only upon those iron rails. What if those rails were taken away? She reasoned, her wrinkled old face expressionless, that the Iron Horse could not pass.

So she obtained a log chain (probably by theft), and taking her lean and scrawny pony, she hitched it to a rail and began to pull up the track. About half a mile of freshly laid track was damaged before the road crews discovered

the old woman and chased her and her pony
away. There was no wreck this time, because
the track was speedily repaired. But the squaw
had hit upon a plan that caused trouble later.

That June, the grading crews, under rush
orders, worked far ahead of the track-layers. An
inspection party, consisting of General Dodge,
General Casement, General John A. Rawlins,
James Evans the chief surveyor, and several other

dignitaries, rode far ahead of the end of the track to inspect the grades. They also wished to determine the true eastern base of the Rocky Mountains, where the Union Pacific would begin to draw its larger subsidy-loan of $48,000 a mile. Two companies of cavalry, under Lieutenant Colonel J. K. Mizner, escorted them, later augmented by other troops under General C. C. Augur.

On June 28, the party reached Crow Creek, at the foot of the Black Hills. This was designated by General Dodge as a division point for the coming railroad — one of the operating units, where locomotives would be changed, repair shops built, and other details of the work of the line managed when trains once began to run.

The party spent the Fourth of July in camp there, and held a celebration, including a patriotic oration by General Rawlins. It was noted at the time that there was, on that date, only one cabin at the site, the home of an Indian trader.

But, though it had only one dwelling, the future division point at once acquired a graveyard. While the inspecting party was celebrating the national holiday, gunfire was heard to the south. Sioux and Cheyenne Indians were attacking a Mormon grading outfit.

"Boots and Saddles" sounded from the bugles. The cavalrymen leaped on their horses and galloped hard to the rescue. At the sight of the oncoming blue-clad soldiers, the Indians drew off rapidly. The working party was saved, but not before two of its members had been killed.

The two slain men were buried near the solitary cabin, and the spot was named Cheyenne by General Dodge, perhaps in commemoration of the Cheyenne attack so near it. Later it would become a fine city, and the capital of Wyoming.

The episode at Cheyenne was only one of many in that year of 1867, and at last General Sherman awoke to the peril along the Union Pacific route, and personally came to take charge. From Julesburg, Colorado, he wired Governor Hunt of that state:

I am here now and General Augur is across the Platte on the line of the Union Pacific Railway. The Indians are everywhere. Ranchers should gather at stage stations. Stages should bunch up and travel together at irregular times. I have six companies of cavalry and General Custer is coming from the Smoky Hill Route.

GENERAL W. T. SHERMAN

General George A. Custer, to whom this telegram referred, was the officer who later was killed, with all of his immediate command, in the Battle of the Little Bighorn.

As repeated skirmishes continued to be fought by grading parties, far in advance of the tracklayers, orders were given to graders, track men, and bridge men: "Never run when attacked." This was because the wild tribes respected a sturdy defense, while if the white men attempted to flee, they would immediately charge and cut them down. Most of the skirmishes occurred when Indians tried to run off livestock, in which they were all too frequently successful.

Even back along the track, far behind the head of construction, tragedies occurred in that period.

On August 6, 1867, a war party of Cheyennes, led by a chief named Turkey Leg, came down from the north, along an old Indian trail that was crossed by the railroad near Plum Creek, Nebraska. The Indians, who later said they had never seen a train before, watched with astonishment from a high ridge when one roared by.

"Far off it was very small," a warrior named Porcupine later said, in the simple words of a savage. "But it kept coming and growing larger all the time, puffing out smoke and steam, and as it came on we said to each other that it looked like a white man's pipe when he was smoking."

After the train passed, they went down and examined the track. Perhaps word of the exploit of the old Indian squaw had come to their ears, for they said among themselves:

"Now the white people have taken all we had and have made us poor and we ought to do something. In these big wagons [cars] that go on this metal road [the track] there must be things that are valuable. If we throw these wagons off the iron they run on, and break them open, we should find out what was in them and could take whatever might be useful to us."

Two of the warriors, Porcupine and Red Wolf,

got "a big stick" (it was a railroad tie) and fastened it to the rails. They climbed a telegraph pole and tore down some of the wire to get something to tie the "stick" to the track. By so doing, although they did not know it, they created a break which caused William Thompson, head lineman, and a repair crew of five men, to start in a handcar from the nearest station (Plum Creek, five miles away) to investigate.

As Porcupine said later, "Quite a long time after

it got dark [it was about 9 o'clock at night] we heard a rumbling sound, at first very faint. Then the sound grew louder and through the darkness we could see a small thing coming with something on it that moved up and down."

This was the handcar on which Thompson and his crew were riding, worked by the men who pumped up and down on the handles.

At the sight of the fire the Indians had built near the track for cooking, and the Indians themselves, the crew worked harder to speed past the danger. But the handcar suddenly struck the tie that was wired to the track, upset, and threw the men to the ground. They scrambled to their feet and tried to flee. But the Cheyennes came bounding down upon them.

All of Thompson's companions were killed. Thompson himself ran off into the night, pursued by a Cheyenne on horseback. The Indian shot him through the right arm, and then knocked him down with the butt of his rifle. When the white man fell, the warrior dismounted, stabbed him in the neck with his knife, and then scalped him.

Thompson pretended to be dead. "It felt as if the whole top of my head was coming off," he later said. But he did not make a sound.

The Indian leaped on his horse and rode away, and Thompson hid in the darkness. Thus he witnessed the events that followed soon after.

Encouraged by their success with the handcar, the Cheyennes went to work on the track itself. With poles they pried up a rail and bent it upward. Then they piled on more ties and sat down to wait.

Presently they saw the headlights of a freight train coming from the east. It was, in reality, the first of two trains, one running not far behind the other.

In the train's locomotive were Brookes Bowers, engineer, and Gregory Henshaw, fireman. In its caboose were William Kinney, conductor, two brakemen named Fred Lewis and Charles Ratcliffe, and another man described as a "deadhead" (free passenger).

When the train struck the bent rail, the Indians later said, the engine "jumped up into the air and the cars came together." The locomotive was derailed, pulling the tender and five cars off the tracks. Both Engineer Bowers and Fireman Henshaw were killed.

Some of the cars caught fire from the burning engine, and the delighted Indians danced and whooped about it.

The caboose at the rear of the train had remained on the track. Some of the savages shot into it, without hitting any of the men inside, and then left, being more interested in the spectacular fire up front. At that, the four white men jumped from the caboose and hid in the darkness.

All at once Conductor Kinney thought of the second freight which was coming up behind. If it was not stopped, it would ram into the wreck, and its crew would share in the tragedy!

"Go and flag that train behind," he ordered Lewis.

"I don't dare," said the brakeman. "The Indians are all around!"

"Damn the Indians!" cried Kinney. With that he began running down the track with his lantern. In a moment Lewis and the "deadhead" passenger started after him.

Ratcliffe at first remained behind, hiding under the caboose. But after a few moments he saw the legs of an Indian, walking alongside to investigate.

At once the brakeman rolled out on the side opposite and ran for his life after Kinney and the others. The sound he made tearing through the tall grass to reach the track told his enemy what he was doing. With a yell the Cheyenne, joined by another warrior, started in pursuit.

It was a race for life. The Indians had left their rifles behind, or Ratcliffe would soon have been shot down. They were armed only with knives and tomahawks, but they were athletes and could run like the wind. Ratcliffe also could run, and fear lent extra speed to his legs.

Ahead, a mile away, he could see the second freight. He heard the whistle of the locomotive, signaling for brakes, as the engineer spied the frantic waving of Kinney's lantern on the track. If Ratcliffe did not reach that train before the Indians caught up with him, he was doomed.

Behind him he heard the pounding feet of his pursuers, striving to overtake him. At times it seemed he could almost feel the pang of a knife blade between his shoulders, or a hatchet splitting his skull. But he leaped on, panting, and still kept out of their reach.

The train had stopped now, and Ratcliffe saw the other three men climbing aboard. What if it should begin backing away for safety, and leave him to his fate!

He used a little of his precious breath in a yell. Behind him sounded an answering yell from one of the Cheyennes. They were almost on him. He made one more effort, one added sprint.

Then he heard his shout answered from the train.

At the same time the Indians, shrinking from the full glare of the headlight which now beamed squarely on them, dropped back and slipped off into the darkness.

A little later Ratcliffe was hauled into the engine cab and the train began backing toward Plum Creek station.

In the meantime, Thompson, bleeding from wounds in his arm and neck and where the scalp was torn from the top of his head, watched an eerie sight as the Indians broke into the wrecked train.

In the boxcars the Cheyennes found bales of cloth, boxes of tobacco, sacks of flour, sugar, and coffee, ladies' bonnets, saddles, ribbons, velvets, and other articles.

All of these things were strewn over the prairie. By the light of the burning train, Thompson saw Indians fasten the ends of bolts of cloth to the tails of their ponies, and gallop back and forth, unrolling the bolts and leaving them trailing behind, as they laughed and whooped. Women's hats were perched ludicrously on savage heads, sometimes on the heads of horses. Ribbons, intended for pretty feminine furbelows, were wrapped around painted bodies, or used to decorate the manes of ponies.

Now came an even wilder yell. A barrel of whiskey had been found in one of the cars. The savages rolled it out, opened it, and proceeded to get completely drunk. Flames were carried from car to car until the whole train was ablaze, while the intoxicated Indians danced around it,

their wild figures, silhouetted by the blaze, seeming to Thompson to be those of devils.

But the drunkenness of the Cheyennes gave him his chance to get away. At daybreak next morning, hardly able to crawl, he reached Willow station, sixteen miles west. And he survived this terrible adventure, scarred though he would always be.

The Cheyennes, next day, were driven off from the now completely demolished train by Major Frank North and two companies of Pawnee scouts.

This episode was only one of those which occurred along the Union Pacific line. Elm Creek, east of Plum Creek, was attacked by the Sioux, who killed five section hands and ran off all the livestock at the place.

Sidney, Nebraska, was struck by the savages. Two freight conductors, Tom Cahoon and William Edmunson, were fishing in a creek a mile and a half away, when they heard shooting. They climbed up on the bank to see what was happening, and were spied by some of the Sioux.

There followed another race, as the men

mounted and rode for the station, the Indians trying to cut them off.

Cahoon was shot from his horse, scalped, and left for dead. Edmunson reached the station with four arrows sticking into him. The Sioux were driven off and Cahoon was brought in.

Both he and Edmunson recovered, and Cahoon served a long career as a conductor, retiring eventually in Ogden, Utah, where a street was named after him. It is recorded that he "always wore his hat well to the rear of his head, where there was a peculiar bare spot."

These were only a few of the recorded Indian raids and assaults. The next year, 1868, the Cheyennes were punished so heavily by troops in the Arikaree and Washita fights that they ceased being a serious menace, and treaties at Medicine Lodge, Kansas, and Fort D. A. Russell, Wyoming, later insured a right of way for the Union Pacific.

But Indians were not the only tolltakers of life. Sickness — especially pneumonia from working exposed in all weathers — caused many deaths among the rail crews. More than one man was killed in accidents. Furthermore, the laborers were chiefly Irish, and turbulent. There were fights in which men were fatally injured by pick handle or bare fist or other primitive means. The line of the Union Pacific is marked by graves. Nobody will ever know how many lives were lost in the epic struggle to drive the rails west across the nation.

And yet in that year, 1867, in spite of all obstacles and dangers and deaths, the Union Pacific built 240 more miles of track, reaching westward to the Sherman Pass, beyond Cheyenne.

Through Ice, Avalanche, and Granite

6

AND WHAT OF the Central Pacific, forcing its way eastward?

When its construction reached Cisco, California, November 23, 1866, Charles Crocker learned of the westward progress of the Union Pacific. The news was coupled with a boast by the rival company that it would "build to the California line before the Central Pacific got there."

By this time Crocker and his crews had made 92 miles over the hardest kind of country. But by that same date the Union Pacific had finished 293 miles of track.

The gibe about reaching the California line was a fiery challenge to Crocker. He decided to plunge on with the work, winter or no winter, instead of stopping, as he had the year before.

Perhaps he hardly realized the task he had set

for himself and his men, for the winters of the high Sierras were as deadly as the Indians of the plains.

Cisco was fourteen miles from the summit of the mountains, and 1100 feet below it in elevation. To get a railroad line across the backbone of the great range, it was necessary to bore fifteen tunnels, the most important of which, known as Summit Tunnel, was a quarter of a mile long, through solid granite.

This tunnel was started in midsummer of 1866. It was attacked at both ends, and to further speed its construction, a shaft was chipped down from above in the middle, so that work could be carried on in both directions, toward the two ends. Thus, on four faces, Chinese worked shoulder to shoulder, in twelve-hour shifts, patiently and industriously chipping at the rock surfaces.

So intensely hard was the Sierra granite in this area that at times they gained no more than eight inches a day. It took an entire year to drive that quarter of a mile of tunnel through the mountain.

Meantime, the roadbed must be built to the entrance of the prospective tunnel — and beyond it. Crocker set his stoical squads of Chinese at the task. Up the long, terribly difficult grade from Cisco they toiled, with their picks and shovels and black powder, their wheelbarrows and their hand drills.

As early as October the first snows fell, and in the next five months storms were almost continuous. The ground froze and was covered by a white, icy mass, fifteen feet deep and even deeper. Crocker had 9000 men working, but by December nearly half that number were employed merely in keeping the track open so supply trains could come up. In places the drifts were thirty feet deep. Elsewhere the snow changed to solid ice.

Before that dreadful winter was over, even Crocker admitted that it was impossible to work in the open. Many of his Chinese died of sickness or exposure, and thousands, half-frozen and some of them ill, were shipped back to Sacramento to wait for spring.

But others kept on the job, working in the deep cuts and tunnels, especially the Summit Tunnel. Food, fuel, powder, and construction materials, all had to be packed over the deep snow, usually on the backs of men.

By January, 1867, the section between Cisco and the summit was abandoned, and even the camps at cuts and tunnels were buried beneath as much as forty feet of snow. The Chinese dug tunnels from camp to camp, and from camp to work, and for the rest of the winter 3000 laborers "lived like moles, in dim passages far below the snow's surface."

Beyond the summit, where snows did not lie so heavily on the eastern slope of the mountains, work could continue. But even there it was enormously difficult.

Down the Truckee Canyon, on the side toward Nevada, dense forests of huge trees were encountered. Many of these pines were eight feet or more in diameter. They had to be felled on the right-of-way, their huge trunks cut in sections and rolled away — and all this by hand, for there were no power saws for lumbering in that day. The stumps were blasted from the soil with great charges of powder. As for the ground, almost as

hard as the granite itself in its frozen state, it seemed to defy the efforts of the Chinese workers to clear and grade it.

To provision and supply this advance force,
countless tons of material had to be hauled by
sled from Cisco, over the pass, to ice-covered
Donner Lake. It seems almost incredible, but
among the items thus freighted were three locomotives, rails for forty miles of track, and forty
freight cars. Locomotives of that day, of course,
were much smaller than those of today, but even
so the picture of a railroad engine on a huge sled,
with its teams of twenty, thirty, or more horses
struggling before it up the snowy slope, must have
been exciting and picturesque.

From Donner Lake all these articles were hauled in wagons or heavy-wheeled frames down roads which became deep and muddy, to Truckee, California. It was only twenty-eight miles from Cisco to Truckee, but it cost millions of dollars and enormous backbreaking toil by men and beasts for that winter's transportation.

As the winter progressed, on the western side of the summit another fearsome peril appeared — avalanches. So thickly did the snow gather on the steep sides of the Sierra peaks that eventually from sheer weight it often broke loose and thundered down to the gorges and canyons below.

It is hard to imagine the irresistible power and fury of an avalanche, cascading downward at express-train speed, a froth of flying snow looking almost like steam at its front, carrying hundreds of thousands of tons of snow and debris resistlessly before it, ripping off huge trees in its path like grass, an absolute demon of destruction.

In most cases these avalanches wasted themselves harmlessly in remote canyons. But sometimes, a moment after the ominous roar from above was heard, a crew of workmen, a bunkhouse, even an entire camp might go hurtling over the brink, into a deep gorge far below.

It was impossible to recover the bodies of the men thus lost until the thaws of the following spring. And then, to show the faithfulness of the Chinese, it was related that sometimes groups of men were found "with shovels or picks still clutched in their frozen hands."

As in the case of the Union Pacific, there are no complete figures on the numbers of men who lost their lives, in one manner or another, on the Central Pacific that deadly winter.

Pessimists stated that the road, if it ever was completed, would have to be closed for five months of each year. But that next spring the men in charge of construction met the challenge in their own way.

Sawmills screamed, cutting lumber; and swarming carpenters labored at building heavily timbered snowsheds. Eventually these snowsheds, which covered thirty-seven of the highest forty miles, solved the problem of the heavy snow. Trains passed back and forth as though through tunnels, however deep was the white mass above.

By this time the mileage race between the Central Pacific, building east, and the Union Pacific, driving west, had grown intense, and work on the railroad went on whenever and wherever possible. At the first sign of spring, Crocker moved 6000 Chinese to the gap in the line between Cisco and the Summit Tunnel.

It was a terrible task they tackled. First they labored to cut downward to the ground through the thick crust of ice. For weeks they toiled with picks and shovels and wheelbarrows before the roadbed was exposed, and then at times the coolies worked in dim trenches thirty feet deep between towering cliffs of ice. Below the snow and ice they attacked the actual rock and frozen soil of the roadbed itself.

As the spring thaws came, that year of 1867, some sections of the roadbed, completed at such cost and labor, became soft. The ties and rails laid over it sank in the mud, and the rails twisted and buckled so that the whole thing had to be built over again.

On the eastward slope of the Sierras, beyond the tunnel, work was pushed hard toward the level desert of Nevada. The tunnel itself was not completed finally until September, 1867. It was the last major tunnel in the world to be constructed by hand.

When the tunnels were completed and the snowsheds built, supplies and men and machinery could be carried by steam all the way across the Sierras, even in winter, and the rest of the task seemed easier. By this time, however, the Union Pacific, racing westward, had gained an enormous advantage.

In April, 1868, Thomas C. Durant, vice-president of the Union Pacific, sent a telegram to Leland Stanford, president of the Central Pacific, extending greetings from "Sherman's Summit, Wyoming, 8200 feet above sea level." Stanford wired back, "We cheerfully yield you the palm of superior elevation; 7242 feet has been quite sufficient to satisfy our highest ambition."

Though Summit Tunnel was not as high above sea level as the Sherman Summit, the Central Pacific had far greater difficulty crossing it than the Union Pacific had in climbing Sherman Pass. The summit of the Sierras was very much steeper, and almost the whole roadbed had to be cut through solid rock. On the other hand Sherman Pass over the Black Hills was reached more easily, the general elevation of the land being much higher, while the pass itself offered a natural route by which, with good engineering and construction, the mountains could be surmounted.

While the Central Pacific thus chiseled its way eastward through the granite of the high Sierras, the Union Pacific had built mile after mile westward over the prairies of Nebraska and southern Wyoming. It was too late, the heads of the Central Pacific saw, to try to equal the mileage of the rival line. They now wished only to reach Utah as soon as their friendly enemies did, so that they could share the traffic of the populous Mormon colonies surrounding Salt Lake City.

Once across the mountains, Crocker looked over his seasoned building crews and felt a stir of confidence.

"Give me the material I need," he promised his partners, "and I can build a mile a day of completed railroad."

They accepted his challenge, and the materials came to him. Thirty ships at one time were plowing the seas all the way around South America and up to California, with cargoes of iron rails that Huntington had bought in the East. Gangs of expert loggers were at work constantly, providing the timber needed for ties and trestles from the magnificent forests of the Sierras. Other necessities were provided as rapidly, and Crocker went to work.

He built across Nevada, his 6000 Chinese, now expert in their trade, leveling the roadbed. Behind them the track-layers — mostly Irish — labored with speed and efficiency.

Crocker did not try to drive his rails in a straight line across Nevada. He chose the easiest ground for construction. As a result, years later when E. H. Harriman of New York gained control of the line, he had to spend millions of dollars straightening out the snakelike curves Crocker had left, by this means shortening the line considerably.

There were two reasons why Crocker chose the easiest way, however crooked, that required the fewest cuts and fills, the least grading and the minimum of bridges and trestles.

First, there was the question of speed. He had had quite enough of the hard, slow progress through the Sierras. Now that he was in the comparatively level desert, he avoided natural obstacles whenever he could.

The second reason was that he piled up mileage. What difference did it make that the line was not as straight as it might be? Here construction costs were cheap, and every mile built now meant a 100 per cent profit, in government lands and subsidies. If he could not meet the Union Pacific at the halfway mark, Crocker could at least make as many miles as possible in the distance he did travel.

The Chinese, who had nearly frozen in the mountains, now suffered from heat in the desert. Nevada was terribly hot, and alkali dust rose in clouds, burning the eyes and nostrils. But the blue-clad, basket-hatted graders labored on, with their picks and shovels and wheelbarrows, seeming to be tireless, even in the most blistering weather.

Crocker's track-laying was as systematic as the Union Pacific's, and before the race was over his men were to set a record that was long discussed.

Meantime, the Union Pacific, ever pushing westward, was having its troubles. For one thing, as it got farther and farther from its supply point, Omaha, food became a greater problem.

But buffalo herds swarmed on the plains, and the Union Pacific hired a hunter to shoot buffalo for the commissary. His name was William F. Cody (later known as Buffalo Bill), a tall, handsome plainsman, said to be the most expert huntsman in the West. They paid him $500 a month, and for eighteen months he kept them supplied.

Each morning he would ride out, and each day he would bring down ten to twelve buffalo for the day's meat supply. In those months, by his own count, he killed 4280 buffalo. Because of his good looks and spectacular buckskin costumes, he was popular with the Irish track laborers. One of them, in fact, is said to have made up the jingle that gave him his nickname:

Buffalo Bill, Buffalo Bill,
Never missed and never will;
Always aims and shoots to kill
And the company pays his buffalo bill.

The large number he killed seemed at the time to have little effect on the buffalo herds. For a number of years after the road was finished, trains frequently had to halt to permit the huge shaggy animals by hundreds to stream across the railroad tracks ahead. Passengers would amuse themselves by shooting the creatures from car windows. But the railroad actually spelled the end for the mighty herds. Eventually the buffalo would be almost exterminated, and when they were gone the "Indian Problem," as it was called, ended. The plains Indians lived on the buffalo, and when their natural food supply was gone, they had to surrender.

The Union Pacific had its troubles with the weather, too. There were heavy snowstorms in winter on the plains and in the mountains it crossed, and snowsheds could not be built to protect the great stretches that were exposed. Snowplows, mounted on the fronts of engines, were constantly at work during storms, but they could not keep the road open all the time.

One episode illustrates the difficulties and dangers met during a blizzard. A "pilot train," as the snowplow trains were called, stuck fast in heavy drifts during a fierce snowstorm in January, 1869. Though the crew put out signals and lights to warn any other train that might be coming, a passenger train rushing up behind did not see these warnings, because of the blinding blizzard.

It crashed full into the rear of the pilot train, causing a severe wreck.

To their surprise the men of the crew found that the weight of the impact had driven the snowplow through the drift, and the pilot train was able to go on, seeking help. But so heavy was the storm that a rescue train from Laramie, Wyoming, only fifteen miles away, did not reach the wrecked passenger train for more than twenty-four hours. The passengers had suffered in the cold, without food, heat, or light, and some of

them had been badly injured in the collision. Fortunately help arrived before any of them died.

Sometimes the road was blocked for many days at a time, and such delays were serious because they held up supplies for the working crews. The Union Pacific began to hitch as many as eight engines together, to give added power to the snowplow in front. But this weight was too much for the roadbed, it was found, causing the rails to spread.

As a result, the number of engines in a "team" employed for clearing snow was usually four. Another four engines would stand by to help pull out the others if they got stuck bucking the drifts. Wrote one observer:

> It was not unusual to see the lead engine completely buried in the deep cuts. Nothing was visible until the steam had melted a hole up through the drift. Neither was it unusual to see such an engine pulled back clear of the cut with every wheel sliding. It was impossible to move a lever or turn a wheel until the ice had been picked away from the moving parts.

Yet somehow traffic was kept moving most of the time and construction continued throughout the winter.

At last, spring appeared and a new problem confronted the railroad. The snows melted and with the thaws there were heavy spring rains, causing roaring floods in all the watercourses. Time and again bridges were washed away and other sections of track undermined.

On one occasion a stretch of roadbed became so mushy from recent downpours that a whole crew of track laborers had to line it, using crowbars to steady the superstructure while a construction train crept over it. But repairs to this and other broken sections were made as soon as men and materials could be rushed to the weakened points, and the work went on as the railhead was pushed steadily westward.

As they neared Utah, both the Union Pacific and the Central Pacific cultivated the friendship of the Mormons there. Thus they obtained workers for their crews, and food from the farms to feed their men.

One of the strange features of the building of the railroad across the wilderness was the series of "boom towns" that sprang up at the temporary railheads. Every one of them, in its brief life of sudden prosperity, roared day and night.

Counting from the east westward, along the Union Pacific, there arose in turn North Platte, Julesburg, Sidney, Cheyenne, Laramie, Benton, Bryan, Green River, Wasatch, Corinne, and Promontory Point. Counting from the west eastward, on the Central Pacific, there were Dutch Flat, Cisco, Truckee, Reno, Humboldt, Winnemucca, Elko, and Wells.

But the Union Pacific towns were the most notorious. The tough Irish laborers were great drinkers and great gamblers. The Central Pacific's Chinese did not drink, and gambled only among themselves.

Each of the Union Pacific towns thrived for a brief time, until the next railhead was established farther along the line. Then everybody loaded up their belongings — even buildings, which were so made that they could be knocked down and quickly reassembled. All this was placed in railroad cars, or wagons which traveled along the road beside the track, and the new town soon was populated while the old one was left to wither, with hardly anyone left in it. Because of this method of moving, and because of the wild sprees when they were established, the mushroom towns became known as "Hells on Wheels."

These railhead towns were anything but virtuous. They moved so that they could prey on the thousands of laborers in the construction crews. Julesburg, 377 miles from Omaha, proudly called itself "the wickedest city in the world." In June, 1866, Julesburg had a population of just forty men and one woman. By the end of July, that same year, it had 4000 people — a whooping, joking, swearing, carousing, shooting crowd. Dance-hall girls danced all night long with one boisterous partner after another, and saloons blazed with lights through all the dark hours. In the outskirts of the town, hundreds of campfires twinkled where "transients" slept.

Hardly a morning passed without a man being buried — killed in the drunken sprees of the night before. Finally, gunmen and gamblers decided to take the town over entirely. They bullied legitimate storekeepers and hotel owners and even employees of the railroad. Any who resisted were beaten or even killed. Merchants, soldiers, teamsters, graders, tourists, Mexicans, Indians — all had to pay tribute to the racketeers who, with the women who associated with them, "owned" the town.

But the Union Pacific had laid out the town. Far up along the track word reached General Dodge of conditions in Julesburg. He telegraphed General Jack Casement, his construction superintendent, to "go back with his track force and help the officers restore order."

Casement and his tough railroaders did as ordered. That fall he and Dodge visited Julesburg together.

"What did you do, General?" asked Dodge.

"I'll show you," said Casement.

He led the way to a graveyard, and indicated it with a wave of his hand. "They died with their boots on," he said, "but when they were buried there was peace."

In the graveyard were more than one hundred

graves. Just how many of them were there because their occupants fought against Casement and his railroaders he did not say.

All of the towns were rough, and every one almost or entirely disappeared, although some of them later grew again with a steadier population. When Dodge and Casement surveyed Julesburg that fall day, less than six months after it "boomed," it was almost deserted, the population having moved on. There remained "only the graveyard, the station agent, heaps of tin cans, and the undisturbed prairie dogs and ground owls."

Julesburg was typical of boom towns everywhere. While they flourished they made a garish picture on the empty plains. Life was cheap — but nothing else. Money by the tens of thousands of dollars was spent on the gambling tables or in the saloons and on the dance-hall girls.

Bad men came and went. At Wasatch, Utah, in three winter months, forty-three persons were "planted" in the graveyard, and of these only five died natural deaths. At Blue Creek there were twenty-eight killings in thirty days. In that town the smallest coin used in exchange was a silver quarter, called "two bits." Dimes, nickels, and pennies could buy almost nothing and were practically worthless.

As the year 1868 drew to a close, the railheads of the two rival lines were approaching each other so closely that the place where they were to join became a matter of utmost importance. Already the surveyors of the two lines had passed each other, going in opposite directions, the Union Pacific surveying west almost to the California line, while the Central Pacific had its course plotted hundreds of miles east of Ogden, Utah. It was evident that neither of the railroads could use all of that survey, and both sides began to jockey for a meeting place that would give them the advantage of building a few more miles of construction, and thus gain for them the additional government lands and subsidies.

Then came news. On April 10, 1869, after much debate, Congress designated Promontory Point, on the bleak northern shore of Great Salt

Lake, in Utah, as the place where the rival lines should meet and unite.

Promontory Point was exactly 1085 miles from Omaha, on the Missouri River, where the Union Pacific started construction. It was 690 miles from Sacramento where the Central Pacific had begun.

And already it was widely known that the final spike to be driven when the rails were joined, would be of pure gold!

7

IT IS natural for men to vie with each other, and beneath the great official contest of railroad building between the two companies, there had grown up another sort of contest, between the men of those companies, unofficial yet full of interest. The Union Pacific and Central Pacific track-layers began to conduct a private duel, to prove which could lay the most track in any one day.

When the Central Pacific's crews reached the Nevada flats after their rigorous battle through the mountains, Crocker promised his partners a mile a day, and delivered. But shortly Casement, of the Union Pacific, heard of it, and before long his men were laying two miles a day.

The fiery little construction superintendent kept speeding construction during all the time that the

Union Pacific's rails were being pushed west, across the Red Desert, climbing the Continental Divide (which at that point was only a bare plateau, though it was 7164 feet above sea level), and passing through the Bitter Creek Basin, with its poisonous alkali waters and its burning alkali dust.

He got three miles a day from his men, then four miles a day, then five. Newspapers told of the achievements of the Union Pacific. The telegraph carried word to the Central Pacific.

One day Casement's Irish laid six miles of track.

Their triumph was short-lived. Very shortly word came ticking back over the wires: Crocker and his Chinese had laid seven miles of track in one day!

It had now become an open challenge.

"Boys," said Casement to his Union Pacific men, "we'll give them eight miles in one day, unless Crocker cries enough!"

Then, starting at Granger, just across the Wyoming border into Utah, Casement's rugged Irish, before the eyes of some distinguished witnesses, laid seven and a half miles of track — less a few lengths — before the bosses finally called it a day. That was late in October, 1868.

Though the men were nearly worn out by their labors, they were filled with pride and satisfaction at the record they had made.

But back came Crocker's reply to this great effort: "The Central Pacific promises ten miles in one working day."

Impossible! men said. Human beings could not lay ten miles of track in one day!

When Vice-President Durant of the Union Pacific heard of the boast he at once telegraphed: "Ten thousand dollars that you can't do it before witnesses."

"We'll notify you," answered Crocker. But he did not say when he would do it.

The whole Union Pacific organization, and the nation in fact, wondered on what day he would make the attempt to do the seemingly impossible.

At that time the rails, stretching from Omaha, had reached the western mountains, and it was the Union Pacific's turn to struggle and fight with heavy grades, trestles, and tunnels. In the meantime the Central Pacific, which had successfully passed over the Sierras, was having a relatively easy way eastward across the deserts.

Brigham Young sent his Mormons to help the Union Pacific in the last westward push to Promontory Point. In the high mountains a thousand men were at work cutting ties, and Vice-President Huntington, of the Central Pacific, who had come to view his rival's progress, smiled grimly to himself as he saw them labor.

"I met some teams with ties in the Wasatch Mountains," he said, "and asked what the price was. They said $1.75 each. They had seven ties in the wagon. They said it took three days to get a load to the top of the Wasatch Mountains and get back to their work. I asked them what they had a day for their teams and they said $10. This would make the cost of each tie more than $6. I passed back that way one night in January, and I saw a large fire burning near the Wasatch summit, and I stopped to look at it. They had, I think, from twenty to twenty-five ties burning. They said it was so fearfully cold they could not stand it without having a fire to warm themselves."

Figuring twenty-five ties at $6 each, that was a $150 bonfire the track workers had going — a pretty costly warming.

The Union Pacific track crossed the Wasatch summit, went through rugged Echo Canyon, and in Weber Canyon passed a lone pine tree with a sign: 1000 MILES.

That meant they were 1000 miles from Omaha, and therefore only 85 miles from Promontory Point, their goal.

On March 3, 1869, the Union Pacific railhead entered Ogden, Utah, and was met by a great procession with flags waving, a military brass band, the booming of cannon, and a banner reading: HAIL TO THE HIGHWAY OF NATIONS! UTAH BIDS YOU WELCOME!

From this time on, the nation almost stood tiptoe, watching the great race to the finish, as both lines stretched toward Promontory Point.

In those days most people forgot about Crocker's boast. But Crocker did not forget it, and neither did the Union Pacific, although just at that time track-laying records were impossible for its crews in the mountains.

There was other byplay besides track-laying feats.

Both lines had their road-grading crews far out ahead of the end of their tracks.

Between Promontory Point and Ogden the graders met — and passed each other, the Chinese heading east, the Irish heading west. The two grades ran side by side, often on sides of hills where one might be above the other. In such cases the graders — Irish or Chinese — who happened to be above their rivals frequently "carelessly" let a few boulders roll down upon their foes.

At last the Union Pacific Irish went even farther than this. They set a powder blast rather far off of their direct course.

When it exploded, it took two or three Chinese with it, "by accident," and there was mourning in the Chinese camp.

Then, in spite of protests from the Central Pacific, another blast "just happened" to go off, burying several Chinese and sending others fleeing.

But the Chinese were not as inoffensive as they

seemed to be. Presently they set off a blast of
their own, "a little off course." It was a huge explosion which put some Irish in their graves and
injured others.

After that this "sport" ceased by mutual con-
sent. It was too dangerous to be comfortable for
either party.

The rails drew rapidly near to Promontory Point
from each direction. On April 28, 1869, the Union
Pacific was only three miles from its finish line,
and the Central Pacific just fourteen.

On that day Crocker made his announcement, in a telegram to Durant: "Tomorrow we will lay those ten miles."

The cunning Central Pacific boss had waited almost until the last minute.

Long before, he had made everything ready for this mighty effort. The roadbed was graded, the ties all laid out, five long trains filled with rails, spikes, bolts, fastenings and other materials, stood ready to move forward.

At seven o'clock on the morning of April 29, Crocker rode out on horseback before his men and gave a signal by raising his hand.

There was a great yell, and instantly the Central Pacific's top team of rail-layers began one of the most remarkable exhibitions of sustained, speedy, and skillful work in history.

There were eight picked men on the track-laying team, four to a side, powerful, rugged, and trained, each one. Their names have been preserved: Mike Shay, Mike Kennedy, Mike Sullivan, Pat Joyce, Thomas Dailey, George Wyatt, Edward Killeen, and Fred McNamara.

Right behind them, on their heels almost, came

a solid column of Chinese. Outside files worked
with picks, the middle file with shovels, ballast-
ing the roadbed as the tracks were laid upon it.
Another group of Chinese by sheer manpower
pushed the heavy rail trucks forward over the
new-laid rails, keeping up with the advance.

This team of workers had been perfectly drilled
by Crocker. Four rail-layers, with heavy pincers,
seized a rail on each side of the truck, and, running forward, set them down. The gaugers instantly adjusted them, the spikers swung their
sledges unerringly, and the rails were fastened
to the ties while the crack layers raced back to
the truck and returned with new rails.

As soon as a rail truck was almost emptied of
rails, the few that were left were dumped on the
ground and the truck itself tipped to one side
off the track, while a new truck, loaded high, was
rushed forward by its Chinese crew, to take its
place.

Dust rose; an indescribable uproar filled the
air — the sound of men talking and shouting,
the clank of rails and the rumble of unloading.

Charles Crocker's team pushed forward at an almost unbelievable pace.

Each time a squad of four rail-layers lifted a rail, they hoisted 560 pounds, for these were thirty-foot rails, fifty-six pounds to a yard. That meant 140 pounds to a man, lifted repeatedly, and always carried forward at a run. There were eighty-eight tons of rails to the mile, and by the time the ten miles which had been set as the goal were completed, these eight men, by sheer strength alone, must handle 1,970,000 pounds of dead weight in a single day's time.

It seemed beyond human strength. But the crack team knew they were the best and fastest rail-layers in all of Crocker's crews. They were like a well-oiled machine, moving as one man, so accurate that there was little need for gauging the rails after they were laid.

If *they* did not do the job, less expert teams might indeed fail.

The tremendous labor went on. Watchers, sent over by the Union Pacific, timed the rate of progress. They found that the Central Pacific was shoving its rails forward at the rate of 144 feet, five pairs of rails, a minute — a pair of rails every twelve seconds! That was more than a mile and a half an hour — the track actually was advancing almost as fast as a man ordinarily walked.

Panting and sweating, the rail-layers maintained their pace with machinelike speed and precision. But these were men, with human muscles and human endurance. Could they make it?

The Chinese were changed in relays, but the eight track-layers refused substitutes.

All morning the killing pace continued. Men marveled. Rail after rail was laid, gauged, spiked, and another placed beyond it, while the Chinese leveled and ballasted the roadbed.

There were 5000 persons present. Many were working, but most of them, by far, were simply watching this incredible performance. Ten miles in one day? It couldn't be done!

But Crocker and his men did not slow their relentless pace for one instant. Noon came. They still rushed on, fighting for every foot. At last, when his watch showed 1:30 P.M., Crocker shouted, "Lay off!"

The track-layers threw themselves on the ground, gasping for breath. They wolfed their lunches, drinking water in great gulps.

"Six hours and a half," one said. "I wonder how we did."

"Here come Minkler and Strobridge," said another. "Maybe we'll find out."

The two men approaching were H. H. Minkler, the track-laying boss, and J. H. Strobridge, the construction superintendent, who had only one good eye, the other having been lost in a blasting accident in the Sierras. Crocker was not with them. He was acting as host to some of the eminent guests who had come to watch the Central Pacific's mightiest effort. At a luncheon served to these guests, on the camp train, excellent food and champagne were set before them. And also — one Union Pacific official remarked enviously — *fresh strawberries!* Where did they get strawberries in California this early? The Union Pacific had no such delicacies.

Strobridge and Minkler halted where the rail-laying team was resting.

"How are you feeling, boys?" asked the superintendent.

"Fine," said one of the men.

"Want to be spelled?"

"No, by thunder! We'll lay rail till Kingdom Come, and never say quit!"

Strobridge smiled. "If that's the way you want it, we'll be starting in another thirty minutes."

He turned away with Minkler.

"Say, boss!" called one of the men.

"Yes?" Strobridge faced the group again.

"How did we do?"

Again the construction superintendent smiled. "You've done better — so far — than any crew of men ever did before. Boys, you've laid six miles of track since morning. Only four miles to go before quitting time."

Tired as they were, the track-layers gave a cheer. "A half day's record broken already! We're a cinch to do ten miles by night!"

But they were to find the last four miles more difficult than they thought — not because of their own seemingly tireless muscles, but because of the rest of the organization.

Horses were needed to bring up new trucks of rails from the construction trains to the Chinese, who kept pushing them close behind the track-layers so that not a motion need be lost. And this was at a gallop. Horses were needed to haul wagonloads of ties — at a gallop. Horses were needed to transport spikes and bolts and nuts and rail joints — all at a gallop.

The animals were changed every two hours, but the strain began to tell. And nowhere, in that desert, could enough fresh stock be obtained to replace them.

In that single day, in addition to 1,970,000 pounds of rails, the wagon men had to drop at their proper places 3750 rail-joint fastenings, weighing seventeen pounds each, together with 52,000 spikes, 14,000 bolts, and 28,000 nuts. All told, the entire weight of iron moved — and some of it moved more than once — was more than 2,000,000 pounds.

Horseflesh could not stand it. The animals tired, and at length were unable to run. Because they could only go at a walk, the whole operation was slowed down by lack of materials far enough ahead.

Crocker glanced anxiously at his watch.

But Shay, Kennedy, Sullivan, Joyce, Wyatt, Killeen, Dailey, and McNamara, the peerless team of track-layers, wasted not a minute. Forward they surged, every man moving with perfect timing, each carrying his share of the weight of each rail, each stepping exactly right, each measuring with his eye the proper place to take hold of the rail with his pincers, and after the short run, the proper place to deposit the load as if all four men on each rail were one.

The great crowd of men who were watching marveled more and more, and sometimes cheered. Word went to Durant that he was losing his $10,000 bet — *if* the men held out.

They held out. Sheer nerve and muscle completed that epic job.

On, on they went, racing against time. Their working day would end at sunset.

They did not even know it when the ten-mile mark was reached. Instead, they continued their furious pace, driven on by fierce determination, although it seemed that human bodies could no longer stand the strain.

The sun was nearing the horizon. At last it seemed to touch Monument Point in the west, and a moment later sank behind it.

"Lay off!" shouted Crocker.

At that cry the whole great movement ceased, and the men flung themselves on the ground, their shirts wet with sweat, their faces black with grime, panting for breath.

Crocker looked at his watch. It was just seven o'clock. He lifted his hand for silence.

"Boys, do you know how much track we've laid

today?" he asked. For a dramatic moment he paused. Then, "Ten miles — and eighteen hundred feet to spare, on top of that!"

A wild cheer broke from 5000 throats as workers and spectators alike roared their applause. Loudest and most sincere were the congratulations of the Union Pacific observers. They had seen what was almost a miracle come to pass.

For many years, two big signs along the railroad marked each end of that great struggle, reading: TEN MILES OF TRACK IN ONE DAY.

The Golden Spike

8

NEXT DAY both companies completed the short stretch of track from each direction to the meeting place at Promontory Point.

The Union Pacific's riotous Irish, who had boasted they could outbuild any Chinese, were half-resentful. They said, given the chance, they could do better than ten miles — better than eleven.

But Crocker had been too shrewd for them. The cunning Central Pacific boss had waited until, as he put it, "the Union Pacific could not get back at me." Before he began his ten-mile race he made sure that the Union Pacific had no more than three miles to go. There could never be a ten-mile test for the rival line.

One sop of comfort came to the Union Pacific's Irish. They learned the names of the crack track-layers who did the incredible job: Shay, Kennedy, Sullivan, Joyce, Dailey, Wyatt, Killeen, McNamara — Irish almost to a man! Well, it took Irish, after all —

But, on second thought, no one could discount the heroic efforts of the hundreds of Chinese who graded and ballasted the roadbed and carried forward the materials — it certainly was partly their victory, too.

General Dodge had watched Crocker's exploit. "They took a week preparing for it," he said rather sourly, "and imbedded all their ties beforehand."

But nothing could dim the splendor of the feat. Ten miles in one day — it became a sort of monument to Crocker and his "Pets."

There was glory enough for all. The Union Pacific, in one tremendous surge of thirteen months, had laid 555 miles of main track and 180 miles of sidings — 735 miles all told. In a similar period the Central Pacific had laid 549 miles of main track, with about as many miles of sidings as their rivals. It might be said that the records were about even; but it must be remembered that the Union Pacific, during this period, had much the harder task. They had to cross the desert in summer, and snow mountains in winter, while the Central Pacific, with the Sierras behind them, had built across relatively level terrain.

On May 1, both construction crews halted, their railheads at Promontory Point — 1085 miles from Omaha, 690 miles from Sacramento — separated only by one pair of unlaid rails. It was planned to join the lines in a great celebration in which the whole nation would participate.

Both railroad companies sent the majority of their workers back, discharging some, and putting others to work improving the trackage already laid. Promontory camp and Blue Creek station — which was a little to the east on the Union Pacific line — were filled with graders and track-layers who were now idle, their pockets bulging with the wages they had been paid.

Those two shack-and-tent towns saw wild times in the next five days. Gambling tables were jammed, dance halls crowded, saloons packed, day and night. There were the usual fights — with fists, clubs and even guns — and the two camps furnished "a corpse a night."

Meantime, from both east and west, high dignitaries were being speeded to participate in the ceremony, which was set for May 8.

The special train that brought Leland Stanford and his guests from California barely escaped a dreadful disaster. It was following just behind a regularly scheduled train. As it sped eastward down the Truckee grade, some Chinese workers, who had seen the first train pass and did not know of the Stanford special that followed, sent a huge log they had felled on the mountainside above, skidding down toward the track.

The log, fifty feet long and three and a half feet thick, hurtled downward like a projectile, farther than expected. It stopped with a terrific jar in the ditch beside the track, its butt end against the near rail.

At the same moment the Stanford special came speeding around a curve. The engineer saw the danger, and whistled for brakes. But it was too late to stop, and the engine struck the log.

A man who was riding on the "cowcatcher" — an old nickname for the engine's pilot — was badly injured. The engine was severely damaged but not derailed. And the log scraped along the side of the beautifully ornamented car of Leland Stanford, leaving a great gouge in it and shearing off both sets of steps.

It was a very narrow escape for the official party of the Central Pacific. Fortunately the telegraph lines were working. A message, wired ahead, stopped the regular passenger train, to which the Stanford coach, badly scarred but still running, was coupled for the rest of the journey. It reached Promontory Point on May 7, in plenty of time for the festivities scheduled next day.

Stanford, the president of the Central Pacific and former governor of California, looked out with his guests from the car windows upon an ugly landscape and a sordid little shack town, all drenched and forlorn-looking, with a cold, heavy rain beating down ceaselessly. What was worse, the storm was general across the country. Word came presently from General Casement that the Union Pacific officials could not arrive before Monday, May 10 — two days after the scheduled "wedding of the rails" — because traffic was interrupted by high water east of Ogden, Utah.

Stanford sent a telegram to California, announcing that the ceremony must be delayed. But in California all preparations had been made — and to Californians, Saturday was the best day of the week for any celebration. So, on Saturday, regardless of the fact that the rails had not yet been joined, torchlight parades marched, fireworks burst brilliantly in the air, bands played, and speeches were made to signalize the great fact that the state was now connected with the rest of the Union.

This was the beginning of what was almost a

comedy of errors. From first to last, everything connected with the planned ceremonial seemed to go wrong in a manner almost laughable — and quite embarrassing to some of the dignitaries involved.

Stanford ordered his special car taken to a siding at Monument Point, thirty miles west of Promontory Point, where the landscape was a little more agreeable. But some of his guests took an excursion on the Union Pacific line as far as Weber Canyon, and were soaked in a heavy downpour. Wet, tired, and hungry, they returned to the Stanford car, gloomily looking forward to two days of boredom in this rain-lashed desert.

During this wait a bit of byplay occurred which gave the Union Pacific crews at least partial revenge for the ten-mile building record of the Central Pacific.

Both systems wanted to claim Promontory as a terminal. But in order to do so a siding must be laid, to give the successful company title to the station.

The Central Pacific made its plans secretly. On a siding behind Monument Point a construction train was quietly made up, loaded with rails, ties, equipment, and a force of workmen.

Sunday, May 9, the storm clouds began to break and fair weather was in prospect for Monday. During Sunday night the Central Pacific construction train moved forward, its speed timed to reach Promontory Point exactly at dawn.

Everything went according to plan. As day broke on Monday, May 10, the train reached the end of the track.

It was greeted with jeers, catcalls, laughter, and hoots, all with a strong Irish accent.

The Union Pacific had stolen a march and worked all night. Its siding was complete when the Central Pacific crew arrived. Promontory was a Union Pacific terminus.

"There was some chagrin and joking, but no ill feeling," said Sidney Dillon, one of the Union Pacific officers, later.

That day, Monday, May 10, 1869, dawned bright but very cold. Promontory's single street, a mass of liquid mud the night before, froze solid. Nevertheless, the sordid little town decorated its shacks with bunting, and its people turned out in their best garments to see the big ceremony.

The plan was for the special trains to arrive from each direction at the same time; but here again came a hitch. At midmorning the Central Pacific officials were there, with no sign as yet of the Union Pacific officials. President Stanford, Treasurer Hopkins, and Superintendent Strobridge were the most important of the Central Pacific figures. Vice-President Huntington was in New York, and Crocker, who would have loved to see the ceremony, was busy on some necessary business in Sacramento.

Promontory Point, located on a plateau that was bare except for some sagebrush and a few scrub cedars, had an altitude of 5000 feet above sea level. Great Salt Lake, its surface feathered with whitecaps in the stiff, cold wind, lay 1000 feet below the town.

Heights of land, covered with trees, could be seen in the distance. But this place where the "wedding" would take place was barren and cold. People who had gathered to watch the ceremony went inside frequently to warm themselves at stoves in the village shacks or in the railroad cars.

Noon came. Stanford and his guests ate a dinner of which the main course was a platter of delicious roast plovers, shot by the steward that morning. Still there was no sign of the Union Pacific officials. It was most annoying.

One o'clock came — two o'clock. Telegraphers, whose instruments had been set on tables beside the track, began talking over the wires, asking what had happened. Impatience grew in the crowd. To make matters worse, the day, which had started out cold, suddenly grew uncomfortably warm, so that the ice-hardened mud became soft and slushy underfoot.

A squad of Chinese busied itself putting the last touches on the grade between the ends of the rails, setting ties, and preparing the roadbed for the last tie and the joining of the tracks.

At last a train whistle was heard, and soon the Union Pacific special arrived. It contained General Dodge, General Casement, Vice-President Durant, Sidney Dillon, the chairman of the board, and others — including four companies of soldiers, complete with a military band, under Major

Milton Cogswell. The soldiers at once were detailed to keep the crowd back from the central point of interest, while the band prepared to furnish music.

Each railroad company had selected one of its finest engines to participate in the ceremony. They displayed an interesting difference in styles. The Central Pacific liked the flaring funnel-shaped smokestack, while the Union Pacific preferred the straight stack.

Engines were named as well as numbered. Central Pacific's locomotive was Jupiter 90, while that of the Union Pacific was Rogers 119. The western line, by custom, called its engines by their names, while the eastern line referred to its engines by numbers. So on this occasion it was the Jupiter on one hand, and Old 119 on the other. Both were brilliant with highly polished brass decorations of various kinds. The engineer of Jupiter was George Booth; of Old 119, Sam Bradford.

Now officials of both companies gathered at the gap. It seemed that things would go smoothly at last. The sky shone blue, the band played.

Men in frock coats, others in business suits, laborers in work clothes, Chinese in their blue garments and basket hats, soldiers in uniform, Mormon dignitaries in black, settlers who had driven in from miles away, Indians in their native

garb, all combined to make a colorful scene. There were a few women — wives of officials and quite a number of dance-hall girls from the town. Newspapermen and two photographers were present. All watched breathlessly, the reporters

making notes, the cameramen busy taking pictures.

From the Stanford car came the "last tie." It ` was of California laurelwood, polished until its beautiful surface gleamed, bound with silver, and with a silver plate on which was engraved: *The last tie laid on the completion of the Pacific Railroad, May 10, 1869.*

Interesting to note was the fact that it was not "Union Pacific" or "Central Pacific" — it was "Pacific Railroad" on that inscription.

The band blared out a new martial air, and the tie was put in place.

Next the two final rails were to be laid — the one on the north side of the track by the Union Pacific Irish, the one on the south side by proud Central Pacific Chinese.

But just at this moment came another hitch — a comic interruption such as seemed to plague this grave ceremonial, and deprive it of much of its gravity.

As the Chinese carried forward their rail, Colonel Charles R. Savage, one of the two photographers, aimed his huge box camera to catch the act.

Someone cried, "Now's the time, Charlie! Shoot!"

All too well the poor Chinese understood the word "shoot," from many unhappy experiences in the violent, gun-carrying West. They looked around, saw Savage's camera pointed directly at them, supposed it was some kind of a deadly weapon — and dropped their rail, scooting for safety.

The onlookers shouted with laughter. After some little time the coolies were convinced that nobody intended to harm them, and they returned and laid the rail.

The engine whistles shrieked, and the crowd roared out a wild cheer.

Now the final act was to be performed.

The engines and the onlookers fell silent as a prayer was offered by the Reverend John Todd, a Massachusetts clergyman.

Not one, but several spikes were presented to distinguished men who were on hand, every one of them with a speech. One was of Comstock silver from Nevada; another of gold, silver, and iron from Arizona; gold and silver spikes were sent from Idaho and Montana. Each was driven into a previously prepared hole in the laurelwood tie — because of the softness of the precious metals of which they were made — by taps from a hammer in the hands of one of the dignitaries.

At last the true "last spike" was presented. It was all of gold — cast from twenty-dollar gold pieces — and was of regulation size, that is, about seven inches long. On one end was the usual head, on the other the usual point. But on the pointed end a nugget was attached, which was broken off and melted into souvenirs.

On its head was engraved: *The Last Spike.* Each of its four sides carried an inscription. On one: *The Pacific Railroad, Ground Broken January 8, 1863, completed May 10, 1869.* On another side: *May God continue the unity of our country as this railroad unites the two great oceans of the world.* On a third side: *Presented by David Hewes of San Francisco.* On the fourth side were the names of the Central Pacific officers. The estimated value of this spike was $413 at the time; today it would be worth more than $1000.

To Leland Stanford, president of the Central

Pacific, was given the honor of driving this last spike. It was placed in the hole into which it was to be driven. A telegraph wire was attached to it, and another to a silver-headed hammer, so that when hammer and spike came into contact, an electric signal would go out to the waiting world.

In Washington, D.C., a magnetic ball was placed on the dome of the national Capitol, and attached to the telegraphic circuit in such a way that it would fall at the electric impulse of the first blow struck on the golden spike.

In San Francisco a connection was made so that the heavy fire bell in the city hall tower would ring, and a salute of 200 guns would be fired. At Sacramento, cannon were ready to boom. (This would be the second celebration in California within two days, but to a Californian, if anything is better than one celebration, it is two celebrations.)

At Omaha, bands and military and civic companies were drawn up, waiting to parade, with artillery saluting at the signal. In Chicago, another vast parade was made ready.

In New York, the choir of Old Trinity Church

stood ready to sing the *Te Deum,* and the bell ringer of that historic church would follow with "Old Hundred" on the chimes, while 100 guns would be fired. In Philadelphia the Liberty Bell was to speak. In Salt Lake City a huge jubilation was planned. And there were many other observances in other cities and places which awaited the signal.

It was a mighty moment, a historic moment, later compared to the signing of the Declaration of Independence and the landing of the Pilgrim Fathers.

Leland Stanford received the silver-headed hammer. The telegraph sent a warning message: "All ready now. The spike will soon be driven. The signal will be three dots for the commencement of the blows."

The grand climax had come.

Stanford, portly, bearded, and very dignified, fully aware of the importance of the occasion, lifted the silver-headed sledge to "strike the blow that would be heard around the world."

Down came the hammer.

And Leland Stanford missed!

His blow, instead of hitting the golden spike, struck only the iron rail! It was a climax, all right, but it was the climax to all the embarrassing and ridiculous little mishaps that had beset this momentous event.

Some of the crowd may have laughed. But Stanford did not laugh, nor did the other officials.

And after all, it really did not matter. The telegrapher did not hesitate. His instrument clicked instantly.

"Dot, dot, dot," it said, followed by "Done!"

From the Capitol dome fell the magnetic ball, and all across the nation cannon saluted, bands played, parades went into action, and wild rejoicings began.

Stanford stepped back after missing his stroke and offered the silver-headed sledge to Durant. The Union Pacific vice-president accepted it. With great courtesy and tact, he imitated Stanford by striking the iron rail, rather than the golden spike.

Stanford and Durant then shook hands across the laurel tie, while the crowd cheered, and some laughed.

Others were invited to tap the golden spike. It finally was driven in fully by General Dodge, chief engineer of the Union Pacific, and Samuel Montague, chief engineer of the Central Pacific. General Dodge had the honor of the last blow.

Now, with whistles screaming, the two locomotives, Jupiter and Old 119, moved forward across the gap as the officials stepped aside.

Slowly they puffed until their pilots touched. The engineers swung along their sides to their noses, each carrying a bottle of champagne. There were two crashes as the engineers broke their bottles, each on the cowcatcher of the opposite engine. The foaming wine showered the last rails, the last tie, and the last spike.

The nation was joined from coast to coast.

As soon as the engines drew back, a crew of workmen rushed forward and dug out the last tie with its precious spikes, replacing it with one more prosaic.

Right after the workers stormed the souvenir-hunting crowd, and all the ties near the point of the rail union were almost demolished for splinters to take home.

The golden spike is still preserved, along with the silver-headed sledge. But the laurel tie with its silver plate and bands was destroyed in the San Francisco fire of 1906.

That afternoon and night, officials, workers, and the crowd joined in a glorious feast and celebration.

In San Francisco a famous writer, Bret Harte, wrote a verse which began:

> *What was it the Engines said,*
> *Pilots touching — head to head,*
> *Facing on the single track,*
> *Half a world behind each back?*

Perhaps they told each other that a new era had dawned in America, and in all the rest of the world as well.

A Nation United

9

THE FOLLOWING MORNING, May 11, the first transcontinental train from the East roared past Promontory Point on its way to California.

It was cheered by the men of both the Union Pacific and the Central Pacific, for neither railroad really "won" the race. It was a tie, fair and square.

They had reason to cheer in pride at their mighty achievement, for the end of their epic contest marked the beginning of a brilliant new day for all of America.

Before, the United States had virtually been cut in two. Most of the population was in the East. Almost like distant islands — separated from the rest of the country by a wilderness harder and more dangerous to cross in many respects than an ocean — lay the states of California and Oregon, and the Territory destined to become Washington.

But now, at one mighty step, the Atlantic was connected with the Pacific by steel rails which could carry heavy freight and passengers speedily and safely. The hopes of George Washington and Abraham Lincoln, who saw that uniting the nation through transportation was the best way of making it strong, were thus fulfilled.

A California pioneer, who had crossed the plains, deserts, and mountains in 1849, taking six months filled with hardship, privation, and danger to make the trek with his covered wagon and teams, rode back on the train to his former home in the East in six days, gaping in wonder at the speed with which the landscape whirled by.

It is hard today for a traveler in a modern Pullman coach, gliding smoothly over a level roadbed in air-conditioned comfort, to imagine those early trains and their crude accommodations. Passengers at first had to sleep in their seats, although primitive sleeping cars were soon added. The ride was rough and jolting, and occupants of the cars suffered from heat and cold, cinders and smoke. Yet in spite of this the train was such an improvement over a covered wagon, or even a stagecoach, that few grumbled.

There was wild, strange scenery to fascinate the travelers — the mighty plains, the weird deserts, and the majestic mountains. One could see through the car windows antelope and deer, prairie dogs and coyotes, sometimes great herds of buffalo, and Indians picturesquely attired.

At eating time a train would stop at one of the way stations where passengers were given thirty minutes to get food in a restaurant operated by the railroad. Meals cost one dollar, and the customer had a variety of strange and delicious dishes — antelope steaks, buffalo roast, elk, bighorn sheep, venison, mountain trout, wild ducks or geese, prairie chickens, grouse, plovers, quail, and other game, all cooked to perfection by skilled chefs. A typical breakfast included: "Eight dishes (for each customer), containing hot beefsteak, two slices of cold roast antelope, a piece of cold chicken, a couple of boiled potatoes, two ears of sweet corn, stewed tomatoes, fruit, and last but not least, four buckwheat cakes, laid on top of one another with syrup to pour over them."

Since breakfast usually is considered a "light"

meal, one wonders what was served for the "heavier" meals of dinner and supper.

From the beginning, passenger travel between East and West was heavy. Freight was carried across the continent at speeds and in volume undreamed of before. One of the first shipments from California was a large package containing tea from China, as a symbol of the "opening of the Nation's trade with the Orient."

But far greater than the carrying of commerce from Asia, no matter how rich, was the importance of the railroad in developing the West itself.

The Union Pacific spent $90,000,000 and the Central Pacific $75,000,000 in building their roads. That was a total of $165,000,000, of which the government furnished $65,000,000. The rest was raised by private loans and sales of stocks.

All this required gigantic financial activities. But that is another story, for this book is concerned only with the building of the railroad.

Some timid economists were alarmed at these expenditures, which were enormous for that day.

Predictions even were made that the country might go bankrupt because of them.

But they need not have feared. Almost from the very first the immense values of the project were evident.

The nation grew wealthier.

Nobody can compute the countless billions of dollars by which America was enriched through land values in what was once worthless wilderness, but now was opened up for farms, cities, towns, industries, and the production of natural resources. The Pacific Railroad showed the way. Very soon the Southern Pacific, the Atlantic & Pacific (now the Santa Fe), and the Northern Pacific were built to the Pacific Coast, while other railroads crisscrossed the West. Each of these made available millions upon millions of acres of land for agriculture, together with lumber, mining, and other sources of wealth which could never be reached before.

The nation grew bigger.

Railroads sent agents abroad to induce people to come and take up the new lands. By hundreds

of thousands hardy and industrious families came
from Europe to settle. With the American population, which also spread into the West, they built
towns and tilled farms, peopling the empty in-
terior. In ten years, from 1870 to 1880, the population of the country grew by almost twelve
million.

The nation grew mightier

With its two coasts knitted together the Union

became a powerful reality. Railroads made the country safe, because it was easier to defend in case of war. The people did not grow different in customs and thinking because of isolation. Instead they mingled together as transportation became easy, and all America was as one, working shoulder to shoulder in harmony and understanding.

Today the United States is the greatest of all

the world's countries. With its gigantic military power it has rescued other, older nations in time of war. With its abounding wealth and generosity it has saved them from poverty and collapse in time of peace.

One important step toward that great goal was taken on the wind-swept Utah flats, when America was made a nation truly and eternally united, by the spike of shining gold.

INDEX